BEGINNING
SONGWRITING

WRITING YOUR OWN
LYRICS, MELODIES,
AND CHORDS

To access audio visit:
www.halleonard.com/mylibrary

Enter Code

3794-8706-6841-3781

ANDREA STOLPE
WITH JAN STOLPE

Berklee Press

Editor in Chief: Jonathan Feist
Vice President of Online Learning and Continuing Education/CEO of Berklee Online: Debbie Cavalier
Assistant Vice President of Marketing and Recruitment for Berklee Media: Mike King
Dean of Continuing Education: Carin Nuernberg
Editorial Assistants: Emily Jones, Eloise Kelsey
Cover Design: Small Mammoth Design
Author Photos: Jon Hastings, Paper Submarine
Recording: Vocals by Andrea Stolpe; Instrumental Performances and Engineering by Jan Stolpe, SonicArt Productions

ISBN 978-0-87639-163-1

1140 Boylston Street
Boston, MA 02215-3693 USA
(617) 747-2146

Visit Berklee Press Online at
www.berkleepress.com

Study with

■ **BERKLEE ONLINE**

online.berklee.edu

DISTRIBUTED BY

HAL•LEONARD®
CORPORATION
7777 W. BLUEMOUND RD. P.O. BOX 13819
MILWAUKEE, WISCONSIN 53213

Visit Hal Leonard Online at
www.halleonard.com

Berklee Press, a publishing activity of Berklee College of Music, is a not-for-profit educational publisher.
Available proceeds from the sales of our products are contributed to the scholarship funds of the college.

CONTENTS

ACKNOWLEDGMENTS

Throughout my songwriting career, I have been fortunate to stand in the shadows of the greats. Pat Pattison and Jimmy Kachulis echo throughout the text of this book. Their ideas, which came before my own, are the solid ground upon which this book stands.

I am deeply grateful for the extent of the contributions of my editor, Jonathan Feist, an accomplished author, composer, and educator in his own right.

I wish to thank my songwriting students, both online and in the classroom, and all the incredible writers I have had the pleasure of coaching over the years. Through your passion for song and willingness to work at your art form, you have taught me about the soul of songwriting.

Finally, I would like to thank Bruce Smith, Phoenix Lazare, Maya Cook, and Ocea Goddard for their beautiful writing that contributed immensely to this book and the inspiration of songwriters everywhere.

INTRODUCTION

I hope you're reading this book because you love music and want to make the creation of it a bigger part of your life. I have always been deeply affected by music, and specifically, songs. The chance to share that appreciation with others keeps me writing songs, teaching in the classroom, and leading workshops on songwriting all over the world. I believe anyone can write songs, even without prior knowledge of how to write or play music. But excelling at anything involves practice and learning good technique. This book is meant to help beginning writers gather technique and form a daily habit of writing.

 Go to www.halleonard.com/mylibrary to access the accompanying audio, and enter the code found on the first page of this book. This will grant you instant access to every example. Examples with accompanying audio are marked with an audio icon.

HOW TO USE THIS BOOK

Each chapter includes writing activities, listening activities, and/or group activities and audio examples. So that you can hear the songwriting techniques at work and so that the sound reflects what you may also hear as you write with your instrument, we have intentionally left some audio examples bare with only a piano. Other examples, however, begin with a solo piano and build into a more full production, so that you can hear how your song using the same techniques might sound when arranged for more instruments.

I encourage you to refer back to these activities often, making them a part of your writing process. As you practice, you'll form your own process of writing that works for you, and it may be different than the process that works for someone else. Use this book as a workbook, either as you write on your own or study with a group of writers interested in gaining more songwriting tools.

Have fun. Remember that creating art is a process, and at times, that process will bring all kinds of feelings from frustration to exhilaration. It is natural to sometimes hate and love writing all at the same time. Allow yourself to feel both, and know that it sometimes takes courage and strength to express our art. But life without art is life without soul. Take heart that you are contributing to the vibrancy of life with the art you dare to create.

BEGINNING YOUR JOURNEY

I can think of a few reasons why you may have picked up this book. Maybe you want to write songs as powerful as the songs your favorite artists sing. Maybe you've always wanted to write music, maybe even had a few piano or guitar lessons, but was never guided in how to combine words and music to create a song that reflects how you feel and think. Maybe you've been writing songs for awhile now, and you want to find out how far you're able to grow as a writer with some tools and techniques. Whatever your reason, music means as much to you as the most profound experiences of your life. And the possibility of expressing yourself through music is an urge that keeps bubbling up to the surface.

There is a good chance that no one close to you has studied how to write songs, much less written songs that they feel capture their true intent. Most people who do write do it by inspiration alone and wouldn't know where to look for guidance on how to write any other way. Songwriting, like other art, is driven by inspiration. But inspiration can be guided by skill, and skill is developed by practice. The more you write, the better you'll get. Natural talent can make you a good artist, but natural talent plus daily practice and learning good technique will make you a great artist.

Even if you have no musical skills yet, you can begin to write songs. Without being able to read a note of music, you can begin to write powerful lyrics, sing catchy melodies, and use various tools to lay down a groove and build a song. Many times, the challenge is simply believing that you have something to say. This book is written to help you define what you want to say, and express it in a way you'll be better understood.

SONGWRITING IN A COMMUNITY

Music is a gateway to the heart. Many people, especially young adults, feel music deeply, in awe of how it captures our deepest feelings that are overwhelming or hard to understand in day-to-day living. Writing songs can be a way we process growing up, at any age. Being writers and creators of art comes from a desire to express what is on the inside, and that expression can be precious to loved ones if listened to with attentive ears.

If you've ever created art or been a lover of art yourself, you know that sharing your inner self with those around you can be exhilarating, and also scary. When we create, we put a piece of ourselves into what we've created. It can feel as if that piece of our self is being evaluated and then judged. When someone shares music with you, try to be aware of your response. Attempt to understand what your fellow artists want to express through sharing the art with you. It may be an excitement for an original idea, or relief in the ability to express feelings, or even simply the desire to be seen and heard. The motive may not be clear for the songwriter, but it can be clear for you. Aim to use the open expression of your fellow writers as a means for connecting with and nurturing each other.

When you are learning songwriting, it helps to have mentors. I am so grateful for the music teachers I have had over the years. Through elementary, middle, and high school band and orchestra and classical piano lessons, I developed a love of music that was nurtured by highly skilled instructors. Some of these instructors crossed over into popular music styles, sequencing and production, and songwriting as a means for teaching music to a younger, more tech-savvy generation. I am forever indebted to them for being open and willing to meet me where my interests laid.

I have structured this book with the intention of helping songwriters learn—even if they are without prior knowledge of how to write and teach songwriting. The writing and listening activities in this book are suggestions for sparking creativity, both for independent songwriters and for those learning together in groups or even classrooms.

If you are leading a songwriters group, whether using this book as a guide, or some other way, allowing songwriters to "workshop" songs—performing them in rough form for each other—gives us experience sharing our art and helps us to create community amongst peers. Creating a safe space for songwriters to share is imperative in nurturing our art. Arranging chairs in a circle, dividing songwriters up into smaller groups for more intimate sharing, and flexibly going with the flow when students interpret writing assignments in their own way help to create this safe and creative space. When we write and share songs, we practice becoming aware of and sharing deeper feelings.

Sometimes, songwriters test that safe space, with explicit lyric content or excusing themselves from sharing or even putting little effort into finishing an assignment. Be cautious in judging each other's motivation, and instead focus on encouraging our fellow songwriters to continue opening up to inspiration. A small bit of encouragement can let each other know that our tangled feelings are accepted.

Music can mean much more than we sometimes think. Music is a place of safety, of retreat, and for some of us, it takes time to share that place with others.

CHAPTER 1

What Inspires You?

Every great song begins as an idea. Have you ever sat on a bench and watched people go by, and made up stories about their lives? Have you ever watched a movie, read a book, or overheard friends talking, and a word or title caught your ear that would make a great chorus? Have you ever awoken in the middle of the night with an idea and quickly recorded it into your phone before falling back asleep so that you wouldn't lose it forever? This is inspiration. It's like a hummingbird that flits into your view for a split second, and you quickly snap a picture before it's gone because you know that in some way it's extraordinary. You may not know how, just yet, but you know and feel there's something special about it.

ACTIVITY 1.1. FEELING INSPIRATION

The feeling you get when you're inspired may feel like a rush through your body, pins and needles, or a bolt of lightning from your head to your toes. Some people describe the feeling as "being in the flow," or when our thoughts are spinning. For you, it may feel different still. Close your eyes for a moment, and remember a time when you felt inspired. Describe that feeling, and where in your body you notice the feeling emerge.

Try to become aware of how this initial instinct feels as often as possible. This is your "writer's instinct," and it tells you when you're expressing something important to you. Over time, our doubts about whether our ideas are really good or not can shadow this valuable instinct. Keep allowing yourself to give this instinct a voice as you practice writing.

As songwriters, we can find inspiration just by living daily life. About the only thing that keeps us from feeling inspired, is choosing not to feel at all. Inspiration requires that we open up to feeling. Feeling scared and angry because we watched our parents have a major fight can give us inspiration. Feeling devastated because we missed the chance to say goodbye to a good friend can give us inspiration. Feeling ecstatic after a first date or ashamed after blowing a job interview can give us inspiration. All of our experiences in life give us inspiration. The way we feel from day to day bubbles up inside until it is expressed through our words and our music, indirectly and directly. This is part of what makes the songs we write unique to us.

The feelings you feel and the way you see yourself and the world around you make your songs a reflection of who you are— the only you there has ever been and ever will be.

ACTIVITY 1.2. THE IDEA NOTEBOOK

A great way to record your inspiration is to carry around an idea notebook. It could be a paper notebook and pen, or it could be on a digital device such as a cell phone or tablet. Record or write down ideas as soon as they come to you. Elaborate on the ideas as much as you wish, writing until the inspiration passes. Try to review your notes later on in the day or before you go to sleep, and write down any additional thoughts. Don't edit as you write, but consider your idea notebook the place where anything goes: good, bad, or just plain ugly.

GET YOURSELF A SONGWRITER'S STATE OF MIND

When we go looking to get inspired, we can help invite the "muse" in many ways. Reading books that interest us, watching movies, experiencing new things, and journaling frequently are ways we feed our inspiration. As writers, we can use these activities to bring on ideas by paying attention to them with what we writers call a "songwriter's consciousness." Having a songwriter's consciousness means that we don't just live on autopilot, but we actively pay attention during these activities to anything we think might spark a song. It may be that we read a few pages with the intent of looking for good titles, or listen intently to the actor's words during a scene in the movie for neat lyric phrases. It might be that we overhear conversations from friends that we think have song potential. Every activity we do in a day holds song ideas. We just have to be alert enough to see them.

BULKING UP YOUR MUSCLES

One of the first challenges songwriters face is figuring out what to do when the inspiration runs out. It can feel great to write a verse and a chorus, the music, lyric, or both pouring out faster than we can write them down. But what do we do when we've said what we want to say and we're only halfway through the song? Similarly frustrating is having a lot of half songs lying around, feeling they're good but losing hope in ever finishing them because we've lost that initial spark.

This is where the tools of songwriting come into play. Without inspiration, we'd never start a song. But without tools, we rarely finish songs. In the next several chapters, I'll take you through a variety of tools to be able to finish the songs you start, know when you're onto something good, and have the confidence to keep going. Think of it like lifting weights in the gym. To get strong, you've got to lift often enough that your muscles get the benefits. The songwriting tools are the weights, and they won't make you a strong writer if you don't get in the writer's gym and lift them often. So grab your idea book, and let's get writing!

How Songwriters Write

There is no wrong way to write a song. Songs are written collaboratively or alone, with lyrics first or music first, over a drum loop or with only an acoustic guitar and an old recording device. Songs are written over the course of fifteen minutes or fifteen years.

Each songwriter should try to find a process for writing that is comfortable for them. It may take some time to determine what process works for you, and sometimes, you might intentionally change your process to grow as a writer and creator of art. To do so, it helps to understand how you typically approach writing a song so that you can see your strengths and know where you can grow.

Below are some of the approaches artists use to write songs.

LET THE MUSIC FLOW

Sitting down with your instrument and simply playing until you hit on an interesting chord or progression of chords can be a great way to start a song. Singing a melody over the top as you play a chord progression lets you focus completely on the music, saving the lyric writing for later. When we write this way, we might sing what we call "nonsensical lyric" while we write a melody. The words we say may be gibberish, the syllables just placeholders for the actual lyric that will come later. Sometimes, that gibberish will resemble words that remind us of ideas we want to use in the real lyric.

If you don't play an instrument, you can still write with this approach. You might sing over a drum loop or a bass, piano, or guitar riff in a program such as GarageBand. Loop the track so that you can sing several passes and get really comfortable with the chords and groove. If you don't have access to technology, you can still write. Clap your hands or snap to create a beat. Or, play the introduction of a song you like (before the verse starts and the artist starts singing), and sing a new melody over that groove. Many great songs have been conceived in the artist's head before ever reaching an instrument. Later, collaborate with a friend who can play chords underneath to complement your melody.

When it's time to write the lyric to your music, consider the mood of the music. If you could describe the music in terms of a feeling, what would that feeling be? Is it happy, sad, anxious, hopeful, aggressive, mournful, victorious, soothing, or bubbly? Add your own adjectives to this list to describe your sound. Then, let those adjectives inspire the mood of your lyric. When the lyric mood and the musical mood agree, the two create a strong union.

ACTIVITY 2.1. MUSICAL AWARENESS

To begin with music, try a simple chord progression. You might choose one, two, three, or four chords stretched out over four or eight bars. Be aware of the tempo you choose without even thinking, and the strumming pattern you settle into, if you play guitar. These choices establish what we call the "groove," and being aware of them helps us to know what grooves we like, don't like, and how to change our style to make different grooves.

If you sing, play around with your voice. Notice where in your vocal range you typically start singing. Is it high, low, or middle? Do you typically sing short, punchy notes with lots of rest space, or do you often sing long melodies stretched out over lots of bars? Just take note of what melody naturally comes out, and try to describe its shape. If you can write the melody down as music notation, do it, and take a look at the basic shape and range. Knowing what you create when you're just playing around enjoying the process helps to understand what makes your song melodies unique, and how you can change them to create something new for another song.

CREATE A SAFE SPACE

When you write, find a place you won't be disturbed. A common worry is that someone will hear us trying out different ideas and judge the strange words, syllables, or notes that may sound ridiculous or "wrong." Concern that someone will laugh at our artistic expression can hamper our ability to come up with ideas. Sometimes, it is a voice inside ourselves that is laughing, judging whether the ideas we might sing would be good or bad. This is a very normal reaction to creativity. The more you can free yourself to express both the notes that sound "right" and the notes that sound "wrong," the more free you will be to write better and better songs.

ON YOUR MARK, GET SET, WRITE LYRIC

If you like to write poetry or stories, you might feel very comfortable writing lyrics first. When we write the words before the music, we are often more focused on what we want to say rather than how well the lyrics fit the melody. But even before we have any music, our lyrics can carry musical elements. We can write our lyrics using rhyme, rhythm, and form that become verses and choruses. We can use tools such as repetition of important lyric ideas, and we can even control elements of music such as lengths of musical phrases and rhyme schemes of a section when we write our lyrical lines. When we write lyric first, we are writing more than just the story. We're making musical decisions too.

Lyrics can be easier to set to music later if they resemble typical song forms, with verses, choruses, and other sections such as prechoruses and bridges. If you like to write poetry, you'll find yourself using some of those same skills to write lyrics. However, lyrics are often different than poetry in that they involve rhyme, rhythmic repetition, and distinct sections that repeat several times. We'll talk much more about these elements in chapter 7.

After you've written part or all of the lyric, you can set it to music. If you don't play an instrument, try starting with a groove on GarageBand or similar software. Singing your lyric over the top of a groove can be fun and a very effective way to write. Try to describe your lyric in terms of the overall emotion. Is the lyric expressing a longing, a sadness, a hopefulness, or a joyfulness? Is it bubbly and happy, or is it reserved and hesitant? Try to choose a drum beat or groove that also feels this way. That will make it much easier to hear the lyric and music connect.

If you don't sing, pay special attention to the rhythm of your lyric as you speak it along with the groove. At times, you may feel like you're rapping. As we'll learn later on, melody is just pitch plus rhythm. Even though you're not using pitch when you speak your lyric, you're using rhythm. This means that you can establish a lot about a melody even if you don't sing. There is one major idea to focus on when you speak your lyric while playing the groove or clapping: listen for the natural shape of the language. The natural shape of the language means the pattern of stressed and unstressed syllables. We don't want the word "happy" to sing as "hap-PY," where "-py" is more emphasized than "hap-." Great rappers know that the language needs to speak naturally, so the listener can focus on what they're saying instead of any awkward way they might say it. When singers sing words, the shape of the words must match the shape of the same words when they're spoken, and when they don't, it must sound completely intentional and serve a purpose for the message and song. This makes sure that the words are believable and understandable.

ACTIVITY 2.2. LYRICAL AWARENESS

To write lyric first, we can write with a pen and paper, type on a computer or phone, or even record ourselves talking about an idea. Begin to form smaller sections rather than long sections of lyric. A typical verse or chorus might be four or six lines long. Try speaking the lyric over a drum loop or chord progression or by simply clapping a beat. This is setting lyric to a groove or a harmonic progression. Alternatively, you could try singing a melody with the lyric, either with or without a groove or harmonic progression underneath and simply clapping or snapping a beat.

When we hear a finished song, it can seem like melody, harmony, and lyric were written all at once. But almost all songs are written step-by-step, with parts of the melody, harmony, or lyric coming faster than other parts, depending on the songwriter's approach.

COME TOGETHER, RIGHT NOW

Many songwriters find the lyric and music come together roughly at the same time. The melody inspires lyric ideas, and the harmony inspires melodic ideas. There may be different points in the song where harmony, lyric, or melody takes the lead and one or the other elements is lagging behind. The beauty in writing these three elements at the same time is that they sometimes feel intimately connected, having been inspired from the same moment. The difficulty in writing all three simultaneously is that they are a lot to manage when inspiration runs dry. By separating the three elements, we make the writing of the song more manageable. Knowing you can break the process down to focus on any one of the three elements at any time can be reassuring and help us feel more in control. Whatever your process for writing songs, starting with your strongest skill—music or lyric—gets you started on the right foot. Sometimes, just having something we love—a lyric bit or a musical idea—can be what we need to get inspired.

IT TAKES TWO...OR THREE, OR FOUR...

A great way to write and have fun is to work with another writer. Collaborations come in all different shapes and sizes. Groups can be two, three, four people—and even more. Some writers in the group may bring lyrics, others may sing, others may play instruments. Whatever the skills the writers bring results in the interesting mix of sounds and personalities that color the song. My rule of thumb is, if I enjoy hanging out with my collaborator, it's a good collaboration. Sometimes, it takes time to get comfortable sharing ideas with another person. Another rule of thumb I write by is an agreement between me and my cowriter that whatever is discussed in the room stays in the room. Even the worst ideas we have are shared in free spirit, in the interest of keeping the ideas flowing.

Later in this book, I'll give you hints on how to find collaborators and start a creative writing group.

TIPS AND ACTIVITIES TO TRY

It can be fun to try a different writing approach and see what happens. Below are just a few suggestions for getting the ball rolling.

ACTIVITY 2.3. INSIDE OUT, OUTSIDE IN

If you normally write lyrics first, try writing music first. If you normally write music first, try writing lyrics first.

ACTIVITY 2.4. COLLABORATION

If you are involved in a songwriting group, organize a collaborative activity. Draw names to pair writers with other writers, or let the pairs form naturally. Try pairing an instrumentalist with a vocalist or lyricist, and suggest ways they might work together using their strengths to guide the writing process. You might also suggest a theme or title or topic to write about.

ACTIVITY 2.5. PHOTOS AND WORDS

A fun activity to do on your own or in a group is to begin writing from a photograph. The song may be sparked entirely from the mood of the picture. Another fun addition is to make a list of words chosen at random. Cut them out and choose one out of a hat to pair with a photograph that inspires you. Try to let the word inspire ideas and even write the word into the song lyric.

ACTIVITY 2.6. MESSAGE IN A CRUMPLE

As a group, an interesting activity can be to ask each member of the group to write on a piece of paper something you'd like to say to someone but are afraid to tell them. Then, have each member crumple the paper up and throw it in a pile in the middle of the group. After everyone has thrown in a paper ball, have everyone choose a ball and unwrap it. Their activity is to write a song using the words on the paper.

ACTIVITY 2.7. GET SPECIFIC

Any activity that focuses a song idea can help get us started writing a song. Trying to write about "love" can leave us feeling like we've got writer's block. Instead, get more specific. Using a photograph, a word or phrase, or as I'll describe in the chapter on lyric writing, a location or object, can spark many more ideas than a broad topic alone.

ACTIVITY 2.8. MUSIC-INSPIRED LYRIC

If lyrics come with more difficulty for you, try choosing a broad lyric concept and moving immediately to your instrument to write music. Try to let music flow that captures the mood of the lyric concept. Record the music you write, in rough form, and set it to repeat. While listening, start journaling on the lyric concept, letting the music inspire lyric ideas. Don't worry about writing actual lyric, but just journal in paragraph form until any lyric words, phrases, images, or concepts come to you that you like.

ACTIVITY 2.9. TIMED WRITING

The perfectionist that lives inside many of us can be a keen editor, but also an annoying and cruel companion. A great exercise to silencing the inner judge can be to limit the time you take to write a song. Each day for two weeks, give yourself forty minutes to write a song. Write the lyric, melody, and harmony in those forty minutes, and record the result at the end of the session each day. What you'll be training yourself to do is write through the process. You will still feel the pain of jotting down a line that you know is cliché, or singing a melody that you feel you've stolen from another song. You may find your chords uninspired. But what you'll also find is that you don't have time to criticize your mediocre ideas. You'll write them down, and move on. This kind of thinking helps us to stay objective as we're creating art, and to create with a spirit of compassion for ourselves.

Song Form and Contrast

Most of the popular songs we listen to have a familiar and definable structure. We call this structure the song form, and there are a few reasons why form is so important. Form helps the listener to know where they are in the song. Form gives the song dynamics: an ebb and flow that carries the listener through moments of tension and release. Without form, the listener wouldn't know what the main message is, sense any forward direction, or believe the singer has any idea what he/she really wants the listener to know and feel.

VERSE/CHORUS FORM

Most songs have at least two parts or *sections*, which we call a *verse* and a *chorus*. The form looks like this:

Verse	Chorus	Verse	Chorus

Sometimes, the song has another verse section. Typically that extra verse happens before the first chorus, like this:

Verse 1	**Verse 2**	Chorus	Verse 3	Chorus

Sometimes, the song has a section that ramps up the emotion after the verse right before the chorus. This is called a *prechorus*.

Verse	**Prechorus**	Chorus	Verse	**Prechorus**	Chorus

Songs can also have a section we call a *bridge*, which happens after the second chorus:

Verse	Chorus	Verse	Chorus	**Bridge**	Chorus

To start the song, we often hear a musical introduction, called an *intro*. To end the song, we sometimes hear a musical *outro*:

Intro	Verse	Chorus	Verse	Chorus	Outro

In the verse/chorus song form, the prechorus and bridge sections, as well as an additional verse, are all optional. Sometimes, we hear songs that start with the chorus section. Other songs move back into a prechorus after the second chorus. Sometimes, song forms break the mold, composed of a single section that repeats over and over. The form of a song depends on how the writer feels the message is expressed best. Though song forms vary, the most basic sections in most songs are the verse and chorus.

There is one other common song form that doesn't involve a chorus at all. This form is a called a *verse/refrain*, as I'll talk about next.

ACTIVITY 3.1. SONG FORMS

Listen to your favorite ten songs from other artists. Pay attention to the different sections, and try mapping out the song form. Were there any song forms that surprised you? If you have been writing songs for a while, consider any song form that you might like to try as you sit down to write your next song.

VERSE/REFRAIN AND OTHER FORMS

Another very common song form is called *verse/refrain* or *AABA*. In this form, there is no chorus section. Instead, there is a refrain that most often occurs at the end of the verse sections and can also occur at the beginning of the verse sections. The refrain is a word or a phrase that summarizes the message of the song. The refrain is often the title of the song, too.

The verse/refrain form is also called AABA to represent the different sections of the song. "A" is the verse section, and "B" is the contrasting section, sometimes called the "bridge" or, if repeated more than once, the "bridge-chorus." A popular song that follows this form is "Yesterday" by the Beatles.

Other songs use the title several times throughout the verse sections and also in the chorus section. This is a great way to make sure the lyric of the whole song really supports and points to the title. Songs that do this are "Basket Case" by Sara Bareilles, "Good Girl" by Carrie Underwood, "Gravity" by John Mayer, and "Summer" by Calvin Harris.

Songs that use a chorus rather than just a refrain are sometimes easier to remember because we hear the chorus section several times. It is also a more popular choice for expressing high-energy lyrics. Verse/refrain forms work well for story songs, or expressing concepts that involve a lot of words. Still, a great idea is to try writing the same song idea with both forms, experimenting with what results in the strongest song.

Activity 3.2. Name That Form

Take a listen to some of these popular songs. Try identifying their form as either verse/chorus or as verse/refrain, but list other sections too if you hear them. Check your answers against those outlined here.

Sara Bareilles "Love Song"   John Legend "All of Me"

Paramore "Decode"   Ed Sheeran "Give Me Love"

Answers

Outro
Ed Sheeran "Give Me Love": Verse, Prechorus, Chorus, Verse, Prechorus, Chorus, Chorus,

Lyrical Bridge, Chorus, Outro
Paramore "Decode": Verse, Verse, Chorus, Verse, Verse, Chorus, Instrumental Bridge,

Prechorus, Chorus
John Legend "All of Me": Verse, Verse, Prechorus, Chorus, Verse, Verse, Prechorus, Chorus,

Chorus, Bridge, Chorus
Sara Bareilles "Love Song": Verse, Verse, Prechorus, Chorus, Verse, Verse, Prechorus,

ACTIVITY 3.3. FORM AND FUNCTION

Consider any song lyric idea that you have thought of. Imagine it as a verse/chorus form. What would seem to be the main message and belong in the chorus? What would seem to be the supporting story and belong in the verse? Then, imagine that same song idea as a verse/refrain form or another you've noticed through your listening activities. What could the main message be if you were to say it in just one word or a short line repeated throughout the lyric? Could that be the refrain?

DON'T BE A BORE

Songs have different sections for several reasons. Imagine a song with fourteen verses, one right after the other. How boring that would be! To keep the listener's interest, after a reasonable amount of time, we give the listener something new to listen to. *When* we give them something new depends on how long we think we can keep their attention with the section we're in. There is a very important word we use in songwriting to describe that something new and why we do it: *contrast.*

Contrast describes the difference in sound between two song sections. In later chapters, we will explore some specific tools you can use melodically, harmonically, and lyrically to create contrast. For now, let's look at the big picture and why contrast is so important.

SHE'S DRIVING ME CRAZY

Imagine listening to someone talk about a vacation they just took. As the person goes on and on and on about the long lines at the airport, the snacks on the airplane, the four-hour flight, the rough landing, the drive to the hotel, the smell of smoke in the room, the over-stuffed pillows, the room service menu, and how he forgot his phone charger, you eventually lose interest. After awhile, you start to wonder if this person has a point!

The point here is, our songs need a point too. The point, in songs, is the chorus (or refrain). The chorus or refrain tells the listener what is the main message, and why the song was important to write and sing.

Now imagine listening to someone talk about that same vacation, and every sentence is like this:

> *"I'm so relieved I was able to take this vacation and come back to my real life. I'm just so relaxed now. I mean, I feel like I'm a new person. I'm not worried at all. I'm just calm and refreshed. It's so great to feel this way. All I want is for this feeling to go on forever. You know, vacations are great for that. It's like fresh air and all I have to do is breathe in, and I'm right where I want to be."*

Right about this time in the story, I'd want to scream "I get it already! You had a good time!" Too much reiteration of the same point begins to sound patronizing, like a lecture, and the language remains shallow. It's like all this big language makes us skeptical about whether the talker is hiding the real substance, or even aware of what's really true.

Both of these examples show an important point about songwriting. Songs aren't made up of only tiny details or big summarizations. They are made up of a bit of both.

In songs, we need detail to tell the story and to put the listener inside the experience. The detail makes the story come alive. But we also need big language to summarize the point of telling all that small detail. So what we can learn is that small detail is great for writing verses, and big summaries are great for writing choruses. This is how the language of the verse contrasts with the language of the chorus.

The main point becomes the chorus/refrain.

The details of the story become the verse.

Other song sections such as prechoruses and bridges contrast in important lyrical ways also. Their contrast can be more subtle, and we'll talk about that in chapter 7.

MELODIC CONTRAST

Each section of a song has a distinct melody. Melody refers to the notes the singer sings. Many songs have a similar shape to their melodies from section to section. Remember our verse/chorus song form? The verse melody is often lower in pitch, where the chorus is often higher in pitch. The bridge sometimes takes the melody even higher, while another common contrasting tool is to take the melody lower again to give the last chorus a bigger punch.

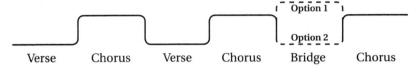

| Verse | Chorus | Verse | Chorus | Bridge | Chorus |

FIG. 3.1. Melodic Contrast

There are other contrasting tools we can use to distinguish song sections melodically. Changing the lengths of our notes from long to short or short to long, and changing on what beats of the measure we set those notes are powerful contrasting tools. We'll talk about all these tools and more and how to use them in chapter 5.

HARMONIC CONTRAST

The word *harmony*, in terms of songwriting, refers to the chords we play underneath the melody. A chord is two (some say three) or more notes played at one time. When we play chords one after another, we're playing the *chord progression* of the song. The chord progression of the verse may be the same as the chord progression of the chorus, or it may be different. Many songs use just a few chords, yet have wonderful contrast between each section. The chords we choose and the order and frequency in which we play them all contribute to the amount of contrast we feel. On the following page is an example of a chord progression for a song and the area where we would feel contrast harmonically.

VERSE	G	C	G	C
	G	C	G	C
CHORUS	D̲	D	C	G
	D	D	C	G

FIG. 3.2. Harmonic Contrast

CONTRAST USING ARRANGEMENT

Song sections use arrangement to contrast in some basic ways. Song introductions generally set the mood for the song, and sometimes carry the melodic "hook" in an instrument such as piano or guitar. When the verse begins, we often hear the groove simplify as the instruments make room for the vocal to enter. The prechorus might involve adding an instrument to gain intensity, and at the chorus, we may hear the full band kick in for that main message to really soar. After the chorus, we might have a short *turn-around*—a few bars of music that resemble the intro of the song and prepare the listener for the beginning of the second verse. Then, the second verse may bring the intensity down again, rising all the way through the second prechorus and into the second chorus. At the bridge, we may hear the groove change entirely, or a breakdown leaving just the rhythm section or even less to provide contrast. Our ears get tired listening to the same intensity and volume for several sections at a time, so musical contrast helps our ears to stay attuned. A song's specific arrangement is also designed to reflect the lyric message of the song. Good arrangers and producers consider what the song is about and what the singer is singing in each section as they arrange the song.

Important Point: Songs can be arranged or produced in many different ways, and it's important to understand what constitutes production and what constitutes the song skeleton. The *production* of a song refers to the kinds of instruments involved and the way in which those instruments play the melody and harmony. The *song skeleton*, however, is merely the three elements of melody, harmony, and lyric. In other words, a song could be arranged in the style of country, pop, reggae, jazz, blues, rock, or other genres. The genre in which it is produced may change, but the chords and basic melody and lyric of the song stay the same. The songwriter is responsible for choosing the chords, the melody, and the lyric. Though the songwriter writes the song, the songwriter may or may not be involved in producing or arranging the song.

Learning to separate production from the song's skeleton is a skill that can take years to develop. As a songwriter, the goal is to write a song that is strong regardless of production or arrangement. When we need to lean on the arrangement to keep the listener interested, we are often dealing with weaknesses in the song's skeleton.

ACTIVITY 3.4. WHAT'S DRIVING?

Pay attention to how your favorite artists' songs are produced. Are the arrangements complex or simple? Do you gravitate towards simple acoustic performances or full band versions? In your own estimation, are the songs you love by other artists driven more by the interesting production, or more by the lyric or melody? Some music is groove-driven, some is melodically driven, and some is lyrically driven. What would you say drives some of your favorite music?

Basic Theory for
Songwriters

Over the years, I have collaborated with many songwriters who don't know how to read music. Some of these songwriters are quite competent on their instruments as well. It isn't necessary to be able to read notes on a staff or know a lot of music theory to write, though a basic foundation can give us more confidence, insight, and expertise, and help us to communicate more easily with each other. Good musical instincts can guide us better than intellectual theory knowledge alone, which is why many writers end up coming to theory after already having played music for several years.

Traditional music theory can be intimidating, both in the material and in the way it is taught. If you've had some piano lessons or had some music theory instruction and decided it wasn't for you, don't sweat it. There is an approach to teaching and learning theory that I believe is more relevant to songwriters, and when broken down into manageable terms and studied for a few weeks, isn't too difficult to digest.

In this chapter, I'm going to try to explain some basic music theory for the purpose of equipping the songwriter with tools to write better, faster, and more creatively. As with any tool, it takes time for it to become habit—so second nature that it simply supports our inspiration while we write. As with other chapters, I'll provide some listening and writing activities so that you can practice the theory tools in bite-sized pieces.

IT STARTS WITH A CHORD

Let's start by imagining you're sitting down to write a song. You've got your instrument in front of you, and you're placing your fingers on the keys or strings. The first thing you might look for is a chord you like or a string of notes that sounds good to sing. You might even do both at the same time.

A *chord* is two (some say three) or more notes played at the same time. The different chords we play that make up a song section is called the *chord progression*. But we don't just play the chords at any time we like. We have to follow a roadmap for *when* to strum the chords or press the keys. So, when we write notes on a staff, we're showing not only what to play, but when to play the chord and how long to hold it.

NOTE LENGTHS

There are a few note lengths that we should be aware of as songwriters. Figure 4.1 shows their names and what they look like, from longest to shortest.

| Whole | Half | Quarter | Eighth | Sixteenth |

FIG. 4.1. Common Note Durations

To write, record, and perform songs, it isn't necessary to learn how to write music on a *staff*, though having the skill to do so just makes us more knowledgeable about our craft and our art, and may even open up more job opportunities as we gain these skills.

FIG. 4.2. Staff

But knowing the note lengths helps us better understand the connection between things like time signature, phrasing, groove writing, counterpoint, ascending and descending lines, transposition, and how melody and harmony interact.

KEY, TIME SIGNATURE, TEMPO, AND SCALE

Each song we write has a key, a time signature, and a tempo. To understand key, let's first talk about scales. A *scale* is a string of notes played one after another that define the *key*. The two most basic scales are major scales and minor scales. Each has a distinct pattern of *intervals*, or distance between the notes, that makes it major or minor. The distance between a white key and a black key on piano is a half step. When two white keys are separated by a black key, it is a whole step. On guitar, frets are half steps apart.

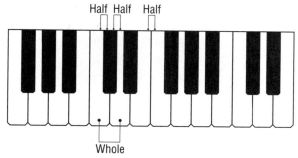

FIG. 4.3. Whole Steps and Half Steps on a Piano Keyboard

When we play the C major scale on piano, we don't play any *sharps* (♯) or *flats* (♭). The sharps and flats are represented by the black keys.

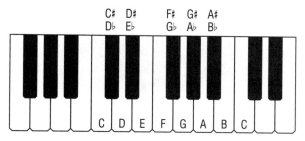

FIG. 4.4. Piano Notes

When we decide the key of a song, we choose the key that involves the fewest sharps and flats so that it is easy to read on the page and easy to play. So for example, let's say the key of a song is D major. Musicians are accustomed to reading two sharps in the key of D major: F♯ and C♯. It's true that F♯ is the same as G♭, and D♭ is the same as C♯. Writing the sharps as flats would indicate the correct notes; however, it would be more difficult for the musician to read. Take a look at figure 4.5. There are twelve major keys and twelve minor keys. Five major and minor keys are written using sharps (G, D, A, E, and B), and five major and minor keys using flats (F, B♭, E♭, A♭, and D♭). One can be written either way (G♭ or F♯). The key of C doesn't have any sharps or flats.

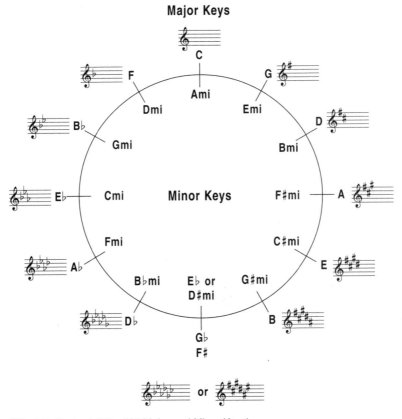

FIG. 4.5. Cycle of Fifths (All Major and Minor Keys)

Whether we choose to write our song in the key of G♯ major or A♭ major is up to us, as long as we stay consistent throughout our *chord chart* or *score*, using sharps in G♯ major, or flats in A♭ major.

ESTABLISHING THE KEY

Now that you know about flats, sharps, and intervals, let's look at how key is established. Take a look at the C major scale in figure 4.6. The key is C because we make a major scale starting from C, or *tonic*, when we play this pattern of intervals. Notice the intervals follow the pattern of whole, whole, half, whole, whole, whole, half. This pattern is what makes it a major scale. That means you can start on any note and play that same pattern, and you'll have a major scale.

FIG. 4.6. Major Scales. Keys of C, G, and D Major.

A minor scale has a different pattern of intervals. Minor scales follow the pattern of: whole, half, whole, whole, half, whole, whole. If you start on any note and play that pattern, you'll wind up with a minor scale.

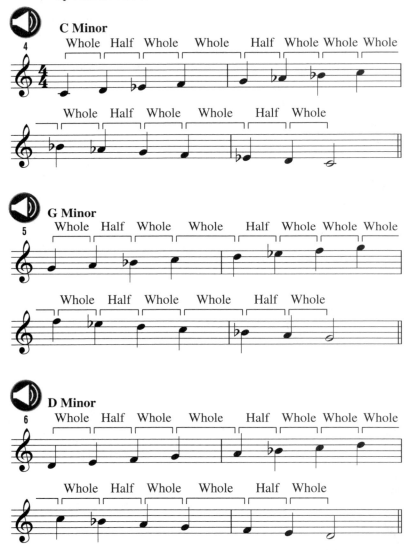

FIG. 4.7. Minor Scales. Keys of C, G, and D Minor.

ACTIVITY 4.1. MAJOR OR MINOR

Set aside your thoughtful brain and just listen for a moment. Try playing a major scale on your instrument and then describe the emotion of the sound. You may have described it as happy or lighthearted or fun or bubbly. Now play a minor scale. Can you hear the difference? Many people describe minor keys as dark, sad, or angry.

COUNT WITH ME, 1, 2, 3...

Another way we talk about the notes of the scale is not by the note names, but by the position of a note in the scale. In other words, we call the first note the root or the "1." The second note of the scale is 2, or "the 2nd." The third note of the scale is 3 or "the 3rd," and so on. We might also use Roman numerals instead of numbers to show the position of the note in the scale, particularly if that note is the root of a chord.

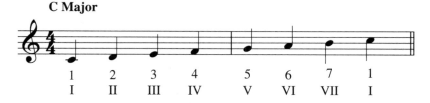

FIG. 4.8. Notes, Numbers, and Roman Numerals

INTERVALS

Labeling the notes with numbers can help us see the interval between two notes. For instance, the distance or interval between the scale's notes 1 and 2 is one whole step. This interval is also called a major second. Between notes 1 and 3 is called a major third, and so on.

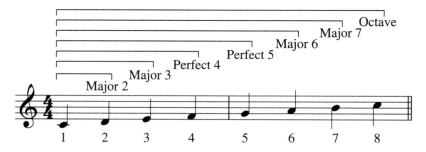

FIG. 4.9. C Major Scale and Its Intervals

Intervals are described as major, minor, perfect, diminished, or augmented. Musicians train themselves to recognize the sound of each interval. This kind of training is called "ear training" or "aural skills." There are some great online tutorials to help us train our ear to hear these intervals, as well as to hear and recognize chord progressions. If this is interesting to you, we recommend the books *Berklee Music Theory* (two volumes, from Berklee Press). Or, you can search online for some beginning ear training tutorials, or ask your instrumental teacher for some suggestions on how to start working on your aural skills.

There are many more scales that are fun for songwriters to play as our ears get more accustomed to hearing them. Harmonic minor scales, pentatonic scales, blues scales, and modal scales are all possibilities to expand our choices and sounds.

TIME SIGNATURE

Time signature is another element of music we choose when we write, whether we're aware of it or not. The most common time signatures we hear in songs are 3/4, 4/4, and 6/8. The time signature tells us how many beats are in the *measure*. A measure is also called a "bar," and helps us hear the regular patterns of musical pulses called "beats." A measure of 3/4 has three beats, and each beat is a quarter note, referred to by the bottom number "4." The pitch here isn't relevant, so we use an "x" to indicate rhythmic value (much like what drummers read on a staff).

7

FIG. 4.10. Two Measures of 3/4

A measure of 4/4 has four beats, with each beat being a division of four, a quarter note.

FIG. 4.11. Two Measures of 4/4

A measure of 6/8 has six beats, each beat an eighth note indicated by the bottom number "8."

FIG. 4.12. Two Measures of 6/8

The 3/4 and 6/8 meters sound very similar. The difference between 3/4 and 6/8 is in how we feel the groove of the song. In 3/4 time, we hear a heavy downbeat on the first of three beats. In 6/8 time, we only hear a heavy downbeat on the first of six beats. The 3/4 meter is often referred to as "waltz time," because it is typical of the waltz feel.

ACTIVITY 4.2. TIME SIGNATURE

Choose ten of your favorite songs and listen for the time signature. Most likely, it is 4/4, but it may be 6/8 or even 3/4. You might also find some songs written in *odd meters*, such as 9/8, 12/8, 5/4, or 7/4. Sting is one of my personal favorites for writing in odd meter. Songs like "Seven Days" in 7/4 and "I Hung My Head" in 9/8 use the odd time signatures to emphasize a feeling of unbalance or "oddness" within the message of the lyric.

TEMPO

10, 11, 12, 13   *Tempo* refers to how fast or slow the song is. We measure the speed of the song in terms of bpm, or *beats per minute*. In classical music, we describe tempo using words like allegro, andante, or adagio. These words refer to a range of beats per minute. So for example, allegro is anywhere between 120 bpm and 160 bpm. When we write our own songs, we often settle into a comfortable tempo. Sometimes, our tempos are very similar throughout all the songs we write, and experimenting with new tempos can be a great way to generate new and fresh song ideas. There are some good metronomes available, the device we use to measure bpm, for computers or phones. Look for one to have on hand next time you're writing and listening to songs.

> ### TEMPO VS. TIME SIGNATURE
> Don't confuse tempo with time signature. Tempo doesn't often change throughout songs, and when it does, it is done by extremely competent players for very specific reasons. Time signatures can change by moving from 6/8 to 3/4, for example, or from 4/4 to 3/4, but the change that is felt is sometimes quite drastic. Remember to keep it simple, not relying on drastic changes like speeding up or slowing down the song or changing time signatures, but on creating contrast using tools of melody, harmony, and lyric.

ACTIVITY 4.3. TEMPO

Listen to a few of your own original songs. Try clapping to the tempo as you listen. Are the tempos the same from song to song? If so, are your strumming patterns or rhythms on piano also the same? What if you tried a much faster tempo, or a much slower tempo next time you sat down to write; how would your strumming patterns need to change? Could you learn a new groove or strumming pattern inspired by this new tempo?

ACTIVITY 4.4. SETTING A PHRASE AT A TEMPO

An interesting brainstorming activity is to take a word or phrase you think might makes a good title and speak it over a very slow tempo, such as 75 bpm. Try speaking the word or phrase using quarter notes and half notes. Listen intently to the message that seems to be behind the word or phrase. Is it sad, regretful, thoughtful, desperate, longing, brooding? Now, speed up the tempo to 136 bpm. Speak the title using quarter and half notes again. How do you hear the message now? Is it lighter, hopeful, bubbly, driven? Maybe frantic, excited, aggressive, or panicked? Tempo affects message.

CHORDS AND SCALES

When we write a song, unless we intentionally change keys, we write the whole song in a single key. This means that we use chords and melody notes from the scale of the key we choose. When we use the chords that belong to the scale, we're using chords *diatonic* to the scale. The chords that are diatonic to the key of C major are easy to figure out if we know the scale.

Let's practice identifying the chords that are diatonic to the keys of C and G. To do this, we'll be playing *triads* (i.e., three-note chords) to show the 1, 3, and 5 of the chord, and using a piano keyboard to illustrate this.

Chords are built on the notes of the scale. Using your right hand to play the first chord in the key of C, play C in the bottom with your thumb, E with your middle finger, and G with your pinky, like this:

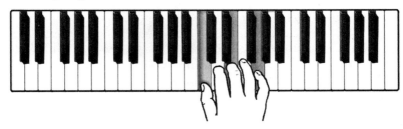

FIG. 4.13. C Major Triad

This is a C major triad. It is the root, 3, and 5 of the C major scale played all at the same time.

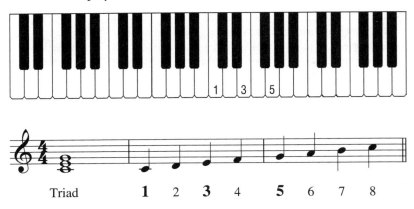

FIG. 4.14. C Major Scale with C Major Triad

Now, we're going to play the next chord in the key of C major, which is D minor. We make this chord by starting on the 2 of the C major scale, D, and using it as the new root of the chord. On top we'll stack the 3 and 5. Using your right hand again, play a D in the bottom with your thumb, F with your middle finger, and A with your pinky.

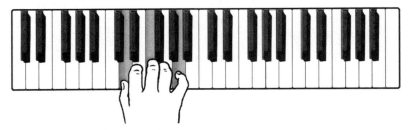

FIG. 4.15. D Minor Triad on Piano

Now, instead of searching for the position of each finger, I recommend practicing the formation your hand takes when you play any triad. We can call this the "claw form," and notice how it stays the same whatever triad in the scale you play. You can practice it by keeping your hand in the same shape as you move up or down the scale, playing all the triads in the key.

14

CHORDS AND VOICINGS

Each chord has a root—a fundamental note, which we call the "root of the chord." In a C major chord, the root is C. In a D minor chord, the root is D. The root is often sounded by the bass player in a band. Sometimes, the other musicians choose not to play the root of the chord on the bottom, but move it up on top of the chord. When we do this, we are playing a different *voicing* of the chord. The voicing of the chord can change the color or feeling of the chord, and is a wonderful tool to use as your instrumental skills grow.

Below are the triads diatonic to the key of C major, meaning, they only use the scale notes in the chords.

15

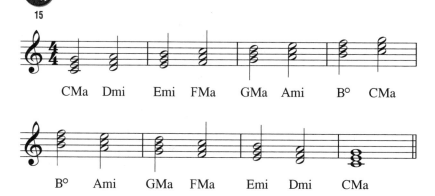

FIG. 4.16. C Major Diatonic Triads

Notice how the D minor triad is minor because the scale tells us to play an F instead of an F sharp. A minor chord is minor because the distance between the root and 3 is a minor third, or a whole step plus a half step. A major triad is major because the distance between the root and 3 of the chord is two whole steps.

FIG. 4.17. D Minor vs. D Major

Again, trust your ears. You can often hear whether a chord is major or minor by how it sounds and feels to you. If the triad is light and happy, it's major. If the triad is dark and sad, it's minor.

Below are the chords of a G major scale:

FIG. 4.18. G Major Diatonic Triads

If you'll compare the two scales, you'll see that the minor and major qualities of the scales match. In other words, the chord starting on the root is major, while the chord starting on the 2 is minor. The chord starting on the 3 is minor, while the chord starting on the 4 is major. Playing triads starting at the root of any major scale results in the exact same pattern of major, minor, and diminished chords. So if you're heading to your piano or guitar to find the chords that are available to you in the major key you're writing in, you just need to remember the pattern:

1	2	3	4	5	6	7	1
Major	Minor	Minor	Major	Major	Minor	Diminished	Major

FIG. 4.19. Triad Qualities for All Major Scales

THE DIMINISHED CHORD, OR "THE WEIRD UNCLE"

There is one chord in a major key that doesn't sound particularly happy or sad, but more suspicious, confusing, or even simply "wrong." This is the diminished triad that results by playing a triad starting on the 7 of the C major scale, the B. When we stack the B, D, and F, we call it a B diminished chord, or Bdim for short.

FIG. 4.20. B Diminished

This chord isn't used frequently in popular songwriting styles, though it does have its purposes. I'll talk a little about other types of harmony you can experiment with as you get more comfortable with music theory and your instrument, but for now, don't let that awkward diminished chord scare you. It's a great chord for highlighting a musical moment, but often isn't a good foundation for creating a stable groove or chord progression.

MINOR KEY CHORDS

Remember how a minor scale has a different pattern of intervals? Minor scales follow the pattern of: whole, half, whole, whole, half, whole, whole. Let's work with the simplest minor scale of all, A minor, which has no sharps or flats.

FIG. 4.21. A Minor Scale

Now, let's build our triads off the minor scale and see what the pattern of minor to major and diminished chords is:

17

Ami	B°	CMa	Dmi	Emi	FMa	GMa	Ami
1mi	2°	3Ma	4mi	5mi	6Ma	7Ma	1mi

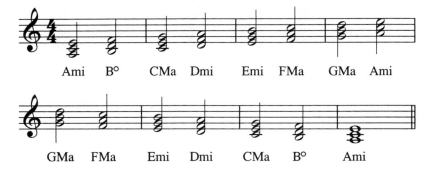

FIG. 4.22. A Minor Diatonic Triads

Take this pattern and apply it to a minor scale starting on any other note, and you'll be playing the chords diatonic to that minor scale. Below are the triads built off the D minor scale.

18

Dmi	E°	FMa	Gmi	Ami	BMa	CMa	Dmi
1mi	2°	3Ma	4mi	5mi	6Ma	7Ma	1mi

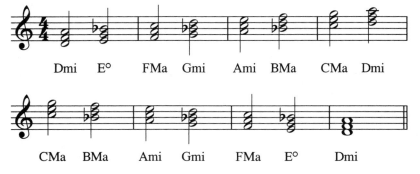

FIG. 4.23. D Minor Diatonic Triads

WRITING CHORDS DOWN

When we write charts for musicians to play, we use shorthand or symbols to indicate the quality of the chord.

- Major chords are written in any of the following ways: C, CMa, CMaj, CM, CMajor, C△. For major triads, the suffix is usually not indicated.

- Minor chords are written in any of these ways: Cminor, Cmi, Cmin, C–, Cm.

- Diminished chords are usually written "dim" or with a circle (°).

There are other kinds of chords too, such as augmented chords or "aug" (or +) and half-diminished chords or mi7♭5 (or ⌀). Still other chords start with a triad, then stack a note or notes on top, such as a 7 or 6 or ♭5. Sometimes, the notes stacked on top are called tensions, and can create chords like CMa7(9).

If you're interested in delving into jazz theory, you'll enjoy learning about and applying those kinds of chords.

MOVING OUTSIDE THE KEY

There are times when we want to search for chords outside those that are diatonic to the key. Sometimes, we want to highlight a lyric moment in our song by using an unexpected chord. Other times, we just want to try some unique and interesting harmonic progressions that inspire us and break old harmonic habits. When we use chords outside the key, we often do it sparingly. The trouble with chords outside the key is that they are outside the key! They take the listener's ears away from the tonic, and destabilize or simply throw off the tonal center. In other words, the more distant the chord feels from the key, the more contrast we get. We don't want there to be so much contrast that the chord or chords sound like a mistake. We always want them to sound intentional, as if we know exactly what we want the listener to feel and hear.

There is a rich relationship between chords that deserves a lot more time than this short chapter on theory can give it. But, for the songwriter who wants to gain tools, I'd like to go over some of the more typical chord substitutions we hear often in popular songs. There are three words that are important for the musician to know in terms of how chords function in a progression. They are *tonic*, *dominant*, and *subdominant*. These terms describe the movement that the chord creates in the landscape of the progression.

The tonic is the chord based on the tonic note of the scale. In the key of C major, the tonic is C major. Tonic feels like home. It's the resting place. It's the resolution, like the period at the end of the sentence. Tonic means that any forward movement stops, and all tension comes to a resolution.

The dominant chord in any key feels like it wants to resolve to the tonic. That is what makes the chord dominant: because its function is to try to resolve to the tonic. The most obvious dominant sound in the key of C major is the G major chord.

The subdominant in any key feels like it wants to move to the dominant chord, which will take us back to the tonic. It also pulls directly to the tonic. The most obvious subdominant sound in the key of C major is the F major chord.

Now, the thing to understand about subdominant, dominant, and tonic is that they express a feeling of movement. That movement is called a *cadence*. A common cadence is when we play the chord progression:

19

F	G	C
4	5	1

This progression is often referred to as a 4, 5, 1 or IV V I cadence.

In this progression, the F functions as the subdominant, the G as the dominant, and the C as the tonic. But the F isn't the only chord that can function as a subdominant chord. The D minor chord can also give us a subdominant feel:

20

Dmi	G	C
2mi	5	1

This progression is often referred to as a 2 minor, 5, 1 cadence, or a II V, for short.

When we create cadences with our harmonic progressions, we are just using chords to function as subdominant, dominant, and tonic. Here are some other fun cadences to try in the key of C major:

21 A♭ G C

22 E♭ F C

23 A♭ B♭ C

24 Ami G C

25 Dmi D♭ C

26 Emi Dmi C

BORROWED CHORDS: USE THEM, THEN GIVE THEM BACK

A great way to spice up the chords of our song is to move outside the key for just a moment. These chords are called *borrowed* chords, because we're just grabbing them for a brief time and then returning to our diatonic chords. The idea with borrowing chords is that we don't try to use them as a foundation for our harmonic progression, but just to add some interesting color. As with any tool, when we use borrowed chords, we do it to highlight a moment in the lyric, and refresh the listener's interest in the song through that new sound.

But how do we know what chords to choose? We use our knowledge about scales and diatonic chords to recognize which chords are outside the key. We know that the chords that are diatonic to the C major scale are as shown in figure 4.16. (As is more common in music notation, we'll leave out "Ma" for major triads, and use Roman numbers to show the chord degree.)

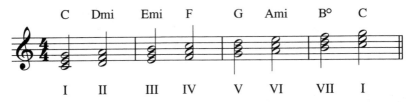

FIG. 4.24. C Major Scale and Triads

If we change the major chords to minor, and the minor chords to major, we get a bunch of chords that don't belong to the key:

C minor

D major

E major

F minor

G minor

A major

These are all chords we could choose from to create an unexpected moment in our chord progression. Many songs we know and love use borrowed chords such as these. Some examples are John Mayer's "Daughters" and Rihanna's "Take a Bow." One of the most popular substitutions used in these songs is the D major chord in place of the D minor chord. Here is a chord progression that uses that movement:

Ami   D   F   C

The D comes as a surprise, and that creates a little more interest for that area of the lyric and melody than the D minor chord may have created.

> **BORROW SPARINGLY**
> It's important to use borrowed chords sparingly and very intentionally when we write. If we use several borrowed chords in a row, the listener can lose sense of where the tonic is, or what the key is. Our chord progression can begin to sound confusing and random. When trying borrowed chords, begin by using only one in place of a diatonic chord in a chord progression.

RELATIVE KEYS

You may have noticed that the C major scale is the same as the A minor scale. Both scales have no sharps or flats. These keys are called *relative keys* because they share the same scale. The roots of the scales of relative keys are separated by a minor third, or a whole plus a half step. You can find relative keys by choosing any note, then counting down one and a half steps for the relative key's root. The lower note is the root of the minor scale, while the higher note is the root of the major scale.

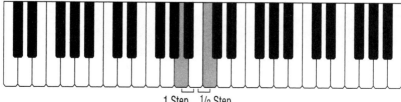

1 Step   ¹/₂ Step

FIG. 4.25. A to C: One Whole and One Half Step

D minor and F major are relative keys, E minor and G major are relative keys, and so on. Using relative keys in our harmonic progressions can be a great way to ensure good contrast between our song sections. In many popular songs, the verse is written using the minor key. For example, this may be our chord progression establishing the A minor chord as the root:

Ami   F   G   Ami

When the chorus arrives, we can use the C major to give lift, brightness, and energy to the song. The chord progression might go something like this:

    C   C   F   F

27

Starting off with the C major gives the first line of the chorus great contrast. Try this technique in your own writing and hear how the chorus gets great energy from the change.

RESOLVING RELATED KEYS

If the verse resolved at any point to C major, we'd then hear the verse in the key of C major. So when you're trying to establish the relative minor as the key, make sure to avoid cadencing to the relative major key until you get to the chorus section.

THEORY AND MELODY

So far, we've talked about how we build chords from scales and can write more interesting harmonic progressions using this knowledge. We can also use our knowledge about keys and scales to write more interesting melodies.

The melody of any song we write uses notes that are taken from the scale of the key of the song. So, if we write a song in the key of C major, the notes we have available to us are the notes of a C major scale: C D E F G A and B. Sometimes, we can look at the melodies of our songs and recognize how we use many of the same notes and intervals throughout all of them. This can be part of our style, but it can also result in many songs that sound the same.

ACTIVITY 4.5. KEY AND STARTING PITCH

Pick three of your own favorite songs. Try to identify the key and the melodic pitch you start singing each section of the song on. Do the same exercise for the other two songs. Do you notice any similarities? Could this be something that holds you back from writing with a fresh melodic sound?

SINGLE CHORD TONE

Some melodies are based on a single chord tone. A *chord tone* is a note that is part of the chord we're playing, and we may use it as our melodic note we sing. These kinds of melodies are very simple, and very memorable. Some songs that use a single chord tone to build a large part of the melody are the verse of Taylor Swift's "Red," Carrie Underwood's "Good Girl," and P!nk's "Try."

 ## ACTIVITY 4.6. MELODY AND CHORD TONES

Play a simple chord progression, perhaps with only two chords, or even a single chord groove. Choose a phrase from your own lyrics or another song you like, and sing it to a single-note melody over your groove. Chances are, you are singing a chord tone in your melody. Try to identify whether you're singing the root of the chord, the 3, or the 5. These are the chord tones.

28, 29

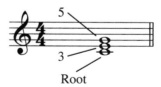

FIG. 4.26. C Major Triad: Root, 3, 5

Now, try singing the lyric phrase using a different chord tone. Notice how often you might settle into using the same chord tones when you write.

NEIGHBORLY NOTES

Another way we can use theory to help write our melodies is to use neighbor notes. *Neighbor notes* are notes just above or below the chord tone we're singing. Neighbor notes are always notes that are part of the scale and key of the song.

Let's say we're writing a song in the key of C major. If our melody begins on an E, the third in the key of C, then our neighbor notes are D and F. Notice how E♭ is not a neighbor note, because it is not part of the C major scale.

CT   LN   CT   UN   CT

FIG. 4.27. Neighbor Notes of E. CT: Chord Tone, LN: Lower Neighbor, UN: Upper Neighbor.

ACTIVITY 4.7. NEIGHBOR NOTES

Many memorable songs use neighbor notes for an instantly catchy effect. Some examples include Taylor Swift's "Red" and Carrie Underwood's "Before He Cheats." Listen to five songs from your favorite artists, and see if you can identify places in the melodies that use neighbor notes as a tool.

ACTIVITY 4.8. WRITING WITH NEIGHBOR NOTES

30, 31

To try out writing with neighbor notes, play a simple chord progression and choose a chord tone on which to start your melody. Try moving your melody up or down to the neighbor note, and then return again to the chord tone. A melody that is this simple has its advantages, being very easy to sing and very easy for the listener to remember.

TWO CHORD TONES

We can also use two different chord tones to write a melody, jumping between them using an ascending, descending, or even zigzag motion. An example of this is when we play a C major chord in the harmony, and move between a G and an E—chord tones 5 and 3—for the melody.

FIG. 4.28. Melody with Two Chord Tones

ACTIVITY 4.9. TWO CHORD TONES

Take a listen to "Dark Horse" by Katy Perry, and Rihanna's "Unfaithful" as examples of two chord tones at work to create a portion of the melody.

ACTIVITY 4.10. WRITING WITH TWO CHORD TONES

Start with a simple one-chord groove. Choose two of the chord tones, either the root and 3, or the root and 5, or the 3 and 5, and jump between the two to write your melody.

PASSING NOTES

Another way our knowledge of scales helps us write melodies is by using *passing notes*. *Passing notes* are notes that connect two chord tones. In the key of C, we might sing the two chord tones E and G, using the passing tone F in between.

CT   PT   CT

FIG. 4.29. Passing Tone. CT: Chord Tone, PT: Passing Tone.

Melodies using passing notes can have an ascending, descending, or zigzag shape.

Ascending   Descending   Zig-Zag

PT   PT   PT   PT

FIG. 4.30. Passing Tone Shapes

ACTIVITY 4.11. PASSING NOTES

Some popular songs that use passing notes to create the melody are "Dark Horse" by Katy Perry, "Before He Cheats" by Carrie Underwood, and "Give Me Love" by Ed Sheeran.

32, 33, 34

Take a listen to these and other songs from your favorite artists, listening for how passing notes are used to create simple and effective melodies.

ACTIVITY 4.12. WRITING WITH PASSING NOTES

Starting with a one-chord groove, sing a short melody that uses passing notes. Notice the chord tone you chose to start your melody on, and whether you decided to use the passing note above the chord tone or below it. Try another melody using the opposite movement, or try starting on a different chord tone for a different effect. You might also try starting your melody on a passing note instead of a chord tone.

ARPEGGIOS

Melodies can also be created from arpeggios. *Arpeggios* are three or more chord tones played or sung in succession. To use this tool, you can start on any chord tone, and move to the chord tone above or below.

FIG. 4.31. Arpeggio and Chord Forms of C Major

ACTIVITY 4.13. ARPEGGIOS

Some popular songs that use arpeggios in the melody are the prechorus of "Love Song" by Sara Bareilles, the chorus of "Ordinary People" by John Legend, and the verse of Rihanna's "Take a Bow." Listen to these and songs from your favorite artists for ideas on how you might use arpeggios in your own melodies.

ACTIVITY 4.14. WRITING WITH ARPEGGIOS

Arpeggios can give a melody a distinct sound, particularly when used to contrast with other melodic shapes. Try combining two melodic tools to write a melody, such as passing notes and arpeggios, or neighbor tones and arpeggios such as in audio examples 35 and 36.

35, 36

FIG. 4.32. Two-Bar Melody with Passing Tone and Arpeggio

A FINAL WORD ON MELODY AND THEORY

It isn't necessary to know theory to write melody or harmony. But, it can be very fun and rewarding when we are able to use it to open up new possibilities for our songwriting. Being aware of what melodic and harmonic choices we typically make can also help us to write something new and different when we want to. Take heart that even when we read and understand theory concepts, it can take a good deal of practice to apply them well without a lot of effort. Take it a step at a time, trying out just one new theory tool for every few songs you write. As you do, you'll become a more versatile musician and skilled writer. But the best result of any tool is that you'll be able to express more accurately and completely what you feel on the inside to others on the outside.

Melody

In chapter 4, we talked about ways you can use knowledge of scales and basic theory to write interesting melodies. In this chapter, we're going to talk about how you can strengthen your melodies without knowing much theory. We'll also talk about tools for creating melodic contrast between your song sections.

Simply put, melody is what the singer sings. It has two elements: pitch and rhythm. Pitch tells us the tone we are to sing, and rhythm tells us how long to hold that tone. In music notation, melody is written using sixteenth notes, eighth notes, quarter notes, half notes, and whole notes, and other subdivisions including triplet eighths, sixteenths, thirty-seconds, and even sixty-fourths. Though it is helpful to read music and understand how the notes we sing are related to the chords we play on our instrument, we can still write songs without this knowledge. The key idea is that we need to trust our ears to tell us when the melody sounds good over the chords we play. For basic theory tips, refer to chapter 4, but for now, let's learn all we can learn by simply using our ears and feeling music instead of writing it down for others to be able to play.

Important Point: Many songwriters can't read music, and still others don't know the chords they are playing or the names of the notes they are singing. What these songwriters do have is an instinct for when the melody feels right. It's true that part of that instinct can come from talent, but another part of that instinct comes from listening intently to other music and practicing the art form of writing.

NOTE NAME BAD, MELODY GOOD

We can describe melody in many ways apart from naming each pitch and duration. For instance, we can describe a melody in terms of its shape, whether the notes are particularly long, or short, and whether there is a lot of rest space between the notes. We can also notice whether the pitches are close together, or if there are large jumps between the pitches. We can describe if the melody starts before or after the downbeat of a measure. We can notice whether the *phrases* are short or long. We can even notice how often a group of notes repeats. All of these ideas can describe any melody we hear or write. And they are all great ways to define why the typical melodies we write ourselves sound the way they do.

The most important characteristic of a melody is its *motive* (or "motif"). The motif defines the melody as belonging to only that song. It is like a fingerprint of the song. It can be one or two notes, or several notes long, but when we hear it, we instantly know what song it belongs to. The motif is repeated throughout the melody of the song. Different sections of the song can carry different motifs.

The most common places in the song to hear the motifs are the first line of the verse, and the first line of the chorus, or wherever the title appears in the chorus. In these areas, the song introduces the melodic idea that makes the song unique, and makes the new section stand out from the previous section.

Most popular songs have strong, distinct melodic motifs. In other words, the songwriter put special effort into writing a melody for the first line of the verse and the first line of the chorus and over the title that was unique and interesting. Many times, the melody that the writer settles on isn't the first melody he or she thought of, but one that took several tries to get right.

Note: The rhythm of a melody can be more important in identifying the motif than the pitches of the melody. We can actually change the pitches but keep the same rhythm, and the motif will still be identifiable. If we change the rhythm but keep the pitches the same, we no longer have the same motif.

ACTIVITY 5.1. THE MELODIC MOTIF

Many songs have easy-to-recognize melodic motifs. Artists and bands with hit singles make their careers on them. Even artists who write less structured songs base their melodies on memorable motifs. Try identifying the melodic motifs that define the verses and choruses of some of your favorite songs. Can you sing them? What do you think makes them particularly memorable? Can you think of any songs you love that don't carry a melodic motif? Listen to them again, and pay special attention to any repeating melodic ideas.

REPETITION, REPEAT

Imagine the melody of a song that had no repetition, but was just an unpredictable string of pitches and rhythms. The melody would be very hard to sing and remember. The reason we become aware of a melodic motif in a song is because that small part of the melody is repeated. The repetition helps us to remember the song melody. Repetition also shows the listener what is the focus, or the main musical message we should hear and understand.

Song melodies tend to use repetition in some common positions in the song. For instance, choruses may consist only of one line, repeated several times. "Your Body Is a Wonderland" and "Say (What You Need to Say)" by John Mayer are examples of this type of repetition. Some songs even use repetition of a single section or melodic motif throughout, creating a very simple song form. Songs like these include "Summer" and "Feel So Close" by Calvin Harris, and Beyoncé's "If I Were a Boy."

Other songs use repetition of the first half of the chorus in the second half of the chorus. Examples include "Life Is a Highway" sung by Rascal Flatts, and "Time After Time" by Cyndi Lauper.

Verses also use repetition of a melodic motif. There are a few common structures for verse melodies involving repetition of just one or two melodic motifs. Take a look at the structures below and the songs that use them:

Structure 1: Exact Repetition of a Single Motif

Line 1: Motif 1

Line 2: Motif 1

Line 3: Motif 1

Line 4: Motif 1

Song examples include "Say (What You Need to Say)" by John Mayer and "Bad" by Michael Jackson,

Structure 2: Alternating Between Two Motifs

Line 1: Motif 1

Line 2: Motif 2

Line 3: Motif 1

Line 4: Motif 2

Song examples of this structure include "Daughters" by John Mayer, "American Woman" by the Guess Who, and "Airplanes" by B.o.B.

Six-line sections use repetition in some typical patterns too. We might hear two motifs, repeating like this:

Line 1: Motif 1

Line 2: Motif 1

Line 3: Motif 2

Line 4: Motif 1

Line 5: Motif 1

Line 6: Motif 2

A song example of this structure includes "I'm with You" by Avril Lavigne.

Remember how I said you can change the pitch but keep the rhythm of the motive and it will still be recognizable? Listen to the verse and chorus of "Sing" by Ed Sheeran. Do you notice how much repetition there is? The pitches change, but the short lengths of the notes are generally the same.

When we repeat a melody, we make the melody memorable. How much repetition can we use before it's too much? There isn't a steadfast rule, but I encourage you to play around with repetition to find what you like. Below is a scale that might help visualize the effects of too little or too much repetition in a song.

No Repetition   **Too Much Repetition**

◄───►

- **Song sounds haphazard, accidental.**
- **The listener doesn't believe the artist knows what he/she is doing**

- **Song sounds trite, simple, forced**
- **The listener doesn't believe the message of the song.**

FIG. 5.1. Repetition Scale

All song sections use repetition, whether it's in the verse, prechorus, chorus, or bridge. Repetition is one of our most powerful tools to focus the listener on what sound and message is most important to the song.

REPEATING MOTIFS WITH VARIATION

Sometimes, melodic motifs aren't repeated exactly, but use a slight variation. The singer may change a note or add or take away a note from the motif to create a fresh sound for that line, or to accommodate the lyric of that line, but the overall effect is still repetition. Try to hear the melody in context of the bigger idea. Is the line meant to reinforce the motif, or to introduce a new and contrasting motif?

ACTIVITY 5.2. REPETITION OF THE MOTIF

Choose one of your favorite songs by another artist, and listen specifically for repetition of the melodic motif. Next, plot out the structure of the verse, counting how many times the motif repeats. Do the same for the chorus motive. How much repetition was used? Choose another favorite song and plot the structure. Do you notice any similarities between the structures of the songs? What insight does this give you about what you enjoy listening to? How could you apply this insight to your own writing?

ACTIVITY 5.3. REPETITION IN THE CHORUS

Try writing a chorus melody using four exact repetitions of a motif. Then, try writing a chorus melody of four lines using two motifs, alternating between them. Notice how comfortable or uncomfortable this kind of simple writing feels to you. How similar or dissimilar to your everyday writing is it? Do you like the results?

THE SECRET INGREDIENTS OF MELODY

Remember the idea of contrast back in chapter 3? Well, without repetition, we wouldn't be able to have contrast at all. Contrast only happens when we've established one sound and want to give the listener something distinctly different. There are a few more tools I'd like to show you that will help you to write interesting melodies and create great contrast between your sections.

Pitch

Remember the drawing from chapter 3 that showed how the melody changes from verse to chorus? Pitch is a very common tool used to create contrast between sections. Many popular songs raise the pitch in the chorus to give the chorus more energy. Songs that are good examples of this are "Sing" by Ed Sheeran and "If I Were a Boy" by Beyoncé. The chorus often uses some of the highest pitches in the melody, because it is the section that shouts out the main point of the song. The verse and prechorus, if there is one, use pitches that are lower, so that the melody has somewhere to rise up from. Simply starting our new section on a different pitch than the most familiar pitch of the section before it can be a great contrasting tool too.

VERSE RANGE

If you often find the choruses of your own songs difficult and too high to sing, look to the verse to find out why. It could be that the verse begins in the middle to higher area of your vocal range. Instead, take the verse down a few whole steps, to sit in the lower area of your vocal range. This will give you more room later on to raise the melody for the chorus.

Note Length

Whenever we write a melody, we are deciding on the lengths of the pitches we sing. As writers, we often gravitate towards the same basic note lengths. We need to become aware of what those note lengths are if we are to change them and do something different. If you've been writing songs awhile, you might wonder why many of your songs sound the same. Or, you might feel that your verses and choruses sound too much alike, and you want to make your choruses more distinct. Changing the note lengths can help solve that problem.

Take a listen to these popular songs that use a change in note length to create distinction for the different song sections. In Taylor Swift's song "22," the prechorus uses suddenly longer notes than the previous verse, and in "Good Girl" by Carrie Underwood, the chorus uses long notes to contrast with the shorter notes of the verse. In "Firework" by Katy Perry, the prechorus and chorus both benefit from longer notes than the verse, while only the chorus utilizes immediate long notes of "All of Me" by John Legend.

The tool is quite simple. Try to describe the note lengths of a section of your song in terms of short, medium, or long. Long notes may last an entire measure, or half a measure, while short notes are just a quick sound. If we use repetition of a motif, our song section becomes characterized by one or maybe two lengths of notes. The key to doing something different is choosing to use a dramatically different length of note in our next section. So for example, our song verse and chorus that uses good contrast might look like this:

- Verse 1: Short notes/medium notes
- Chorus: Long notes ending with just a few medium notes
- Verse 2: Short notes/medium notes
- Chorus: Long notes ending with just a few medium notes

Now, let's say we want to write a bridge melody that contrasts again. We would only need to contrast with the chorus, since that is the section we just came from:

- Bridge: Short notes
- Chorus: Long notes ending with just a few medium notes

CONTRAST

The important idea with contrast is this: When we begin our new section with note lengths that are different than the note lengths that made up the majority of the previous section, we get great contrast.

ACTIVITY 5.4. CONTRAST USING NOTE LENGTH

40

Listen to how different note lengths work to create contrast between the sections of some of your favorite songs. Contrast can occur within a section as well as between sections, but try to see the big picture as much as possible. Do you notice any patterns that might be useful to your own writing?

ACTIVITY 5.5. MELODY WRITING USING CONTRASTING NOTE LENGTHS

Try writing a simple melody using repetition to make a verse. Perhaps it is just a melodic motif repeated four times. Then, describe the lengths of the notes of that motif in terms of short, medium, or long. Try writing a contrasting section to follow your verse using a different length of note. Make sure to use that different length of note right away in the first line of the new section. Do you hear the contrast?

PLACEMENT: BEFORE, ON, OR AFTER

A third very useful tool for creating great melodies is placement. When we sing a melody, where we start singing in relation to the beats of the measure is called the *placement* of the melodic phrase. We can start singing before the chord is played on the downbeat of the measure, at the same time the chord is played, or just after the chord is played.

When we start to sing the melody before the chord is played, the melody is a *pickup* to the *downbeat*.

FIG. 5.2. Pickup Notes

When we start to sing the melody at the same time the chords begin, we are singing *on* the *downbeat* of the measure.

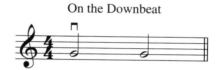

FIG. 5.3. On the Downbeat

When we start to sing the melody after the chord progression begins, the melody starts *after* the *downbeat*.

FIG. 5.4. After the Downbeat

Try listening for the different placements in the song "Just the Way You Are," sung by Bruno Mars. The verse melodic phrases begin after the downbeat of the measure, while the chorus melodic phrases begin as a pickup to the downbeat. Most popular songs will use this technique to help the sections to contrast, along with a change in the lengths of the melodic phrases and a rise in pitch for the chorus section.

Repetition first shows the listener what to expect, so that when we suddenly give the listener something they didn't expect, such as the melody starting on the downbeat instead of before, the sound becomes fresh and new. That's why we place most of the phrases the same way within one section, only changing the placement when we get to the new section.

VARYING PLACEMENT

Remember that we can hear a slight variation of a melodic motif and still hear it as the motif. The same is true for placement. As long as most of the lines in a section start with the same placement, the section can be described as having that overall characterization.

ACTIVITY 5.6. PLACEMENT OF THE PHRASES

If you find your different song sections often sound the same, look at your melodic placement. Could you change the placement in the first line of your new section for more contrast? Try it, and listen to the effect.

41

PHRASE LENGTH: SHORT OR LONG

A *musical phrase* is like a sentence. It has a beginning and an end, and we can hear the pauses between musical phrases like we hear the commas and periods as pauses in speech. Besides pitch, note length, and placement, another way we can describe a melody is in terms of its phrase lengths. A verse may have four melodic phrases that are each two measures long. When we get to the chorus, we can change the length of the phrases to become longer or shorter, and get great contrast.

2-Bar Phrase

FIG. 5.5. 2-Bar Phrase

This melody has a melodic phrase that lasts two measures. Notice how there are no rest spaces breaking the phrase into smaller parts.

But we don't need knowledge of music theory to identify musical phrases. Oftentimes, a melodic phrase lasts as long as a line of lyric. When the singer takes a breath, the phrase may end and another begin. Where the melody uses rest space, one phrase may also end and another begin. Try to rely on your ears to tell you when a melodic phrase is ending and a new one beginning. Trust your judgment, and describe the phrase as short, medium, or long. "Firework" by Katy Perry uses quite short phrases in the verse, where the chorus uses much longer phrases.

We can also glimpse how long a melodic phrase is by how many words fit the phrase. A long line of lyric either needs lots of short notes, or a very long melodic phrase to sing it with longer notes. Just a few words need only a few notes, and possibly a very short melody to sing it.

ACTIVITY 5.7. PHRASE LENGTH

42

Try to identify the lengths of the melodic phrases in a few verses and choruses of your favorite songs. Try to feel the natural pauses in the melody that break it down into smaller pieces called phrases.

ACTIVITY 5.8. CHANGING THE PHRASE LENGTH

Try writing a verse section with long phrases spanning two or more measures each. Then, try shortening the phrase lengths to just one measure long in the chorus section. Do you feel the increase in energy? Now flip that structure, and instead write a verse section with short phrases followed by a chorus with longer phrases. What do you feel now?

CLUSTERED OR INTERVALLIC

We can sometimes describe a melody in terms of whether the notes are close together in pitch, or *clustered*, or involving jumps from one pitch to another, called *intervallic*. An *interval* is the distance between two notes, and if you're into music theory, you know that intervals can be 2nds, 3rds, 4ths, etc. But even if you don't speak music theory just yet, you can notice the overall shape of a melody. If we use notes clustered around the same pitch in a verse, we can switch over to using notes with a larger interval between them in the chorus. "All of Me" by John Legend and "Summer" by Calvin Harris use clustered notes in the verse, contrasting nicely with the choruses that are not clustered. Katy Perry's "Unconditionally" uses an intervallic melodic shape in the chorus, contrasting well with the verse that does not use large intervals between the notes. The greater the change, the greater the contrast.

43

ASCENDING OR DESCENDING

The shape of a melody can also simply be described as ascending or descending. Sometimes, melodies move up or down the scale, such as in the verse of the song "Yesterday" by the Beatles, the prechorus of John Legend's "All of Me," and Rihanna's "Take a Bow." The overall shape of the melody can be a point of contrast when we go against that shape in the next section.

FULL OR EMPTY

There is one final characteristic of melodies that has nothing to do with pitch at all and everything to do with rhythm. Rest space is the time between the sung notes, and gives the melody as much shape as any of the other tools. When we use quite a lot of rest space between notes or between phrases, we create what we call an *empty* sound. Take a listen to the empty sound of the verse of Katy Perry's "Unconditionally." When we load up the melody with lots of lyric and very little rest space between phrases, we create what we call a *full* sound. Now listen to the chorus of "Unconditionally" for the full sound. Bruno Mars' song "Just the Way You Are" uses the opposite pattern. The verse is full and the chorus is more empty with long notes and more rest space in the melody. If every section of the song is full, the song can sound like a never-ending boring lecture of information. If each section of the song is empty, the song can seem too sparse and lose our attention.

ACTIVITY 5.9. FULL AND EMPTY

44

Try writing a section of a song using a lot of rest space, creating an empty sound. You might try one-word lines, or short punchy notes followed by rest space. When you've written a simple section using rest space, try following it with a line or two of a new section with long notes or lots of shorter notes and very little rest space. Do you hear the contrast? What did that contrast do for the energy of the new section?

COMBINING THE TOOLS

Many songs we know and love use several tools at one time. But the important idea here is that the more tools we use at the same time, the greater the contrast we feel. The fewer the tools used, the lesser the contrast. To recap, here are the tools available to use when it comes to writing melodies:

- Pitch: Raise, lower, or add a new one
- Note Length: Shorten or lengthen
- Placement: Before, on, or after the downbeat
- Phrase Length: Shorten or lengthen
- Clustered or Intervallic
- Ascending or Descending
- Rest Space and Empty or Full

By now you might be thinking "Okay, all these tools are nice to know, but how do I actually write a melody?" The answer is, you jump in and try. There really isn't any magic to writing great melodies, except that to write great melodies we often need to write a lot of mediocre melodies first. You might start by singing a pitch, and then moving up or down with the next pitches. You might try changing the lengths of the pitches you sing, experimenting with rhythm. Great melodic motifs are born of a combination of skill and inspiration. It takes a lot of practice and a willingness to write very ordinary melodies before happening upon some great ones. Our creativity thrives when it has room to explore. Let yourself write material that is not your best so that eventually you can write material that is.

Harmony and Groove

Put simply, harmony is chords. Chords are what we play on piano or guitar, or hear established in the bass line. A *chord* is a group of three or more notes. A *chord progression* is a series of chords played one after another.

Many songs have been written using the same basic chord progressions. It often isn't the chord progression that makes the song unique all by itself, but the groove with which the progression is played, and the way the chords interact with the melody. I'll talk about harmony and groove separately, and then talk about how we can use both together to write interesting songs.

THE COLOR OF CHORDS

Some writers enjoy writing the chord progression first. If you play a harmonic instrument such as piano or guitar, you might find that this approach feels natural. Before we even have any lyrical or melodic ideas, we can map out a chord progression that inspires a melody and lyric we want to say. This is especially true if we've got a good groove to go along with our harmonic progression.

When we write a harmonic progression, we first choose the key we're writing in. The key tells us what chords are going to sound natural together, but also what chords are going to sound like they don't quite belong. The idea is not only to choose chords that belong to the key, but to choose chords based on their ability to show the emotion we feel. Sometimes, we choose a chord outside the key to show uncertainty, pain, excitement, or anger. Sometimes, we choose all chords that belong to the key to show certainty, peacefulness, or even boredom. The big idea here is when we put chords together to make a chord progression, they cast a specific emotion. It's our job as the writer to be aware of the emotion our chords are creating, and to send the same message with our lyric.

You can describe the emotion of your chord progression without even knowing what chords you're playing. Is the emotion sad or just reflective? Hopeful or unsettled? Happy or victorious? Angry or confident? It may help to record yourself playing the progression and to listen back another time when your ears are completely fresh. Trust your first impression. If you're still unsure, try playing the recording to two other people. Ask them to describe the emotion they hear.

ACTIVITY 6.1. KEY AND CHORD AWARENESS

Do you find that you write using minor chords a lot? Or, do you tend towards major chords? Are there any keys that you typically write in, possibly because they are easier to play and consist of the chords you know how to play? Try recognizing your typical writing patterns in terms of the keys and specific chords you choose most often. Later, you can use this information to do something different the next time you write a song.

KEEP IT SIMPLE

Many of the songs we love the most are quite simple harmonically. The verse might only have two different chords and the chorus just one new chord. As new writers, there is the tendency to load up a song with every chord we know how to play. But sometimes, more chords just results in a complicated and even messy sound the listener can't follow or remember.

HARMONIC CONTRAST

Remember the word *contrast*? Well, here it comes again, as we talk about harmony. When we write a song, we decide on the chords we'll use for a section—maybe the verse or the chorus. If we use those same chords played at the same rate throughout each section of the song, we wouldn't be able to tell based on the harmony that there are different sections. Each section would sound the same. In terms of harmony, there are two basic ways we can show the start of a new section. The first way is by using a new chord.

That New Chord Feeling

When we use a new chord to start a new section in our song, we are breaking a harmonic pattern that was familiar to the listener. If we wrote the verse using three chords and we start the chorus with a chord the listener hasn't heard yet, the chorus will really sound like a new section. Even if we use one of the three chords that were in the verse, the important idea is that we change the pattern.

Follow the simple *chord chart* below to see how we might create contrast by changing the beginning chord and thus changing the pattern of chords to show the beginning of a new section. Each chord lasts for four beats in a measure of 4/4 time.

45

Verse

G	C	G	C
G	C	G	C

Chorus

D	C	G	G
D	C	G	G

One of the troubles that results from using too many different chords in the verse is that later sections can't generate contrast on new chords alone. Too many chords already create a lot of contrast between themselves, and so the ending sound can be a jumbled mess. Instead, simplify so that each section can focus on creating a specific mood around a defined chord pattern. Below is an example of a chord chart that uses just one chord in the verse. Creating a new sound in the chorus is easy with so much room for contrast.

46

Verse

G	G	G	G
G	G	G	G

Chorus

D	C	G	G
D	C	G	G

ACTIVITY 6.2. SIMPLICITY WITH HARMONY

Try writing a simple song section using just one or two chords. Then, try starting the next section of the song with a chord you haven't used yet. Keeping it simple is a great way to make sure the emotion is clear, and to open up new places to go with the chords of our next section.

Slow Change, Fast Change

Another way we can create contrast between sections is by changing how often we move from one chord to another. If the verse has three chords, and we change chords every two measures, then changing chords every measure in the chorus will definitely make the chorus sound like a new section. Similarly, changing chords every four measures in the new section will make it sound fresh and different.

Changing chords more frequently has a neat effect of giving the song energy at that point. Though the tempo doesn't change, the song seems to bubble over or drive forward with renewed excitement. Changing chords less frequently has the opposite effect, creating a sense of slowing, expansiveness, calmness, or even sluggishness. Just as we choose the type of chords to send a particular emotion, we also choose the rate at which we play them. The rate can have a big effect on the emotion we're creating. In the chord chart on the next page, notice how each chord lasts for one measure, or four beats in 4/4 time.

Verse

G	C	G	C
G	C	G	C

If I change chords more frequently, the chart may look like this:

Verse

G	C	G	C	G	C	G	C
G	C	G	C	G	C	G	C

There, instead of holding each chord for four beats, I hold each chord for two. (The underlines show multiple chords per measure.) This means I'm changing chords more frequently.

I can do the opposite too, changing chords less frequently. That looks like this:

Verse

G	G	C	C
G	G	C	C

Now, each chord lasts for two measures, or eight beats, instead of just four beats.

How much different one section sounds from another depends somewhat on how many tools we use at the same time. For instance, we get a very different sound if we use a new chord at the same time as we change how often we move from one chord to another. But we might get only a slightly different sound if we use all the same chords and just change chords more frequently. When we add to these harmonic tools all the melodic tools for contrast along with lyric tools, we've got endless possibilities for new and interesting songs.

GROOVE, BABY, GROOVE

Many artists approach writing a song from a good groove. The *groove* is the rhythmic feel of the song. What is really relevant to the songwriter is an understanding of how rhythm and groove relates to the overall build or dynamic of the song. I'd like to say a bit about how we can use knowledge of rhythm and groove to achieve good contrast between song sections, energy and richness for our choruses, and overall dynamic that keeps the listener interested all the way to the end of the song. Our groove discussion will also give you an idea of how production and arrangement is used to convey groove.

Straight vs. Swing

Many grooves we hear can be described as either straight or swing. To understand the difference and begin applying these feels to your own writing, take a look at the graphs below.

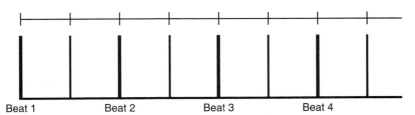

Beat 1   Beat 2   Beat 3   Beat 4

FIG. 6.1. Straight Groove

50, 51

This is an example of a straight groove. Think of this entire picture as one measure. Each of the thick lines are one of the four beats inside that measure. Each one of the thinner lines between the beats are eighth notes. In this straight pattern, the eighth notes are placed perfectly in the middle between two beats. There is no quirkiness here; it's just "straightforward." Audio example 50 shows how this straight feel would sound on a tambourine, while example 51 shows how this straight feel would sound as a loop for our song.

Now, take a look at the graph below of a swing groove.

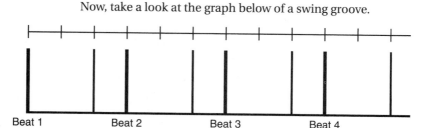

Beat 1   Beat 2   Beat 3   Beat 4

FIG. 6.2. Swing Groove

52, 53

In an absolute swing feel, the space between the beats of a measure is divided in three, and the note that was placed perfectly in the middle of two beats in the straight pattern is now delayed to the last third of a measure. Audio Example 52 shows what this swing groove sounds like on tambourine, and audio example 53 shows this groove using a loop.

You may hear how the level of swing sounds mechanical, as if it is too severe. The example you are listening to is in fact generated by a computer and could not (and truthfully should not) be able to be replicated by a human musician at this mechanical level.

54, 55

It is the human touch that makes swing really come alive. Although the "severity" of a swing pattern is still quite variable from song to song, a swing feel generated by human hand would fall somewhere in between these two placements. Listen to audio example 54 to hear the softer sounding swing pattern on tambourine, and then audio example 55 as a loop.

Again, even this example is computer generated. The precise choice of a swing feel, similar to many Latin-American grooves, is an art all in itself comprised of highly disciplined musicianship and continuous listening that slowly instills an organic feel for this inside the musician's mind. But it's never too late or early to be playful with these choices.

56, 57

For an additional listening experience, refer to audio examples 56 and 57, that utilize drum loops and switches from straight to a more human swing feel, and then to a mechanical swing with perfect division of a beat into thirds.

This discussion around the idea of swing grooves is only the entry to a rabbit hole that goes very deep. Regardless of music genre, musicians make music come alive by purposefully placing notes (or rests) before or after a "mathematically/symmetrically" perfect place. Of course, there is an art and skill to making a conscious decision of placement (rather than the inability to place the note due to lack of practice and/or experience), but you can hear this human, organic type of musicianship on recordings across the board, from John Mayer to Bruno Mars, from Sting to Coldplay, from Sara Bareilles to Aerosmith, and from Michael Jackson to Fall Out Boy.

It is worth mentioning that the masters of hip-hop have capitalized on these concepts cleverly and very musically for decades. As producers utilize samples of real-life musicians playing their various interpretations of a swing feel (many samples dating back to the 1940s to 1970s), then layer different swing patterns with yet another layer of computer-generated grooves, some really astounding rhythmic results emerge. Listen to some more organic hip-hop tracks and for what may even feel like rhythmic oddities when things don't seem to quite line up in a symmetrically divided measure, and then step back, listening to the wholeness of the groove, getting lost in what may seem mathematically off, but feels musically and organically magnetic. Some examples include Lauryn Hill's "The Miseducation of Lauryn Hill" or Jay-Z's "The Blueprint."

RESTS AND RHYTHMIC CHANGES

58

Other ways songwriters can conceptualize groove is to consider rhythm, even while playing a song on a single instrument such as piano or guitar. When we play, we are conveying more than chords alone, but also, the groove with which those chords are heard. Let's unpack that statement further by listening to audio example 58. Listen to the moment we transition from section A to section B. Although the same chords are being played, an increase in dynamic occurs. There are a few tricks that allow section B to gain power, and most of them are based on rhythmic changes.

59

Listening carefully to the bass, you'll recognize that the rhythmic placing in section A is on beats 1 and 3 of the measure. To make this easier to hear, audio example 59 pushes the bass up in the mix.

Though there are some pickup notes too, fundamentally the punch is on beats 1 and 3. Also, notice that there are rests or "holes" in this section. The bass does not play on beats 2 and 4, with some minor pickup notes, but rather takes a breath. Now listen to section B. The bass movement changes dramatically, doubling in rhythm. It is now playing eighth notes throughout the entire section without any rest or "breathing" space at all.

60

Now, take a listen to the tambourine in audio example 60. It too changes its rhythmic value.

In section A, it plays eighth notes creating a very stable beat, almost like the second hand of a wristwatch marching steadily and patiently. In section B, however, it doubles up, now playing sixteenth notes that add a sense of excitement to the section.

Listening again, focus on the piano. In section A, we are playing long, full notes that stay out of the way of a potential melody above it. In section B, the piano plays eighth notes, in a sense quadrupling the rhythmic frequency and therefore the energy.

Now let's listen to the guitars. Although the rhythmic value does not seem to change much between sections A and B, the dynamic is created by something similar we discussed in the bass. In section A, the guitars are playing a part that can be best described as "staccato"—very short. Fundamentally, the guitars here are playing eighth notes, but the character of a staccato note is so short that you can think of it as a sixteenth note followed by a sixteenth rest or breather. Let's try to visualize this:

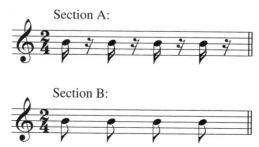

FIG. 6.3. Short Sixteenths vs. Mellow Eighths

When notes flow smoothly into one another without any rests, they can offer us a warm, cohesive, and thick texture that we perceive as dynamically elevated.

Finally, section B uses a classic studio trick, adding another electric guitar part, to really bring the point home. Note, however, that it too locks in with the bass and the piano in their powerful eighth-note groove.

ACTIVITY 6.3. ONE- AND TWO-CHORD GROOVES

A great way to start writing using groove is to keep the harmonic progression simple. Try writing a groove over just one chord. You might choose a key that you feel very comfortable playing in, and start on the root of the key, the tonic. Play the chord using your groove. Now, try adding a second chord to your groove. You might change chords each measure, or change every two or four measures. Notice how even as the chords change, the feel and groove stay the same.

ACTIVITY 6.4. GROOVE AWARENESS

Hearing grooves and being able to play them takes a lot of listening and practicing. But you might be surprised what you can accomplish in just a week or two of immersing yourself in a new groove. Try listening to a style you're not as familiar with for a week. Listen to ten songs a day in this style. After a week, listen to those same songs while sitting with your instrument. Without concern for what chords you're playing, try to express the rhythmic feel of the songs as you play along on your instrument. You could mute the strings if you're a guitar player, or just play one note in the key of the song if you're a piano player. The important idea is to feel the groove, not play the right notes. This exercise can be a lot of fun, and very rewarding for our writing.

ACTIVITY 6.5. RECREATING A GROOVE

Using another artist's song you like, identify the groove, and try to recreate it by clapping or beatboxing. Once you feel comfortable with the groove, imagine writing a new melody and chord progression over it. Let the groove inspire ideas you may never have had without the groove.

ACTIVITY 6.6. OLD GROOVE, NEW TEMPO

Identify another groove you like, and try to recreate it by clapping, beatboxing, or playing it on your instrument. Now, try speeding it up a little, or slowing it down. Play the new groove until you really feel comfortable with it. Now imagine writing a song over this new groove. At the new tempo, what does it sound like it's about? Do you hear any melodic ideas over the groove? How about any chords?

THINKING OUTSIDE THE BOX

Sometimes, when we write, we have another artist's voice in mind, and sometimes, that voice is our own. Even if we have no voice in mind, the way we write can be limited by what our ears allow us to imagine. Sometimes, we write so much like the genre we listen to most that we limit the creative ideas unique to ourselves.

When you feel uninspired or are stuck with a song you can't finish, try to define why. In other words, what genre do you feel the song fits in? Is the singer male or female? Is it a slow song, or an up-tempo song? Then, try imagining the song in another light. If you thought you were writing for a guy, imagine what would happen when a girl sings it. If you imagined the song at a quick tempo with lots of energy, what happens to the message when you slow it down a bit? If you imagined it with a full band, what happens when you look at it as an intimate acoustic performance? Taking a step back to look at our songs from a more objective point of view can help us feel creative again.

Lyric Writing

Almost everybody can sing the words of a few of their favorite songs. If you've got a favorite band or artist, chances are you know many or all the words to every song they've ever released. Song lyrics have an incredible way of expressing the authentic feelings of the singer. They can even capture the beliefs, frustrations, and hopes of entire generations.

It would seem natural that lyrics wouldn't be too difficult to write. After all, we've all been using words to communicate since we learned to talk. On top of that, many popular song lyrics use simple language and lots and lots and lots of repetition. But if you've ever tried to write lyrics, you know just how difficult writing simply and effectively can be.

THE GOOD, THE BAD, AND THE INDIFFERENT

With any art, whether painting, sculpting, or songwriting, it's sometimes hard to judge what is truly "good" and what is not. We might say that "good" art leaves a notable impression on the observer. Or, "good" art is memorable. Or perhaps "good" art is art that has the ability to connect with a large number of people.

As artists practice and mature as artists, our motivation or "why" we create our art becomes more clear to us. Our personal definition of what is "good" may change as we change and grow. So instead of using the word "good" to label our art, I'd like to suggest a few different ways to measure its effectiveness.

Sometimes, we write to express feelings that are meaningful to us. The expression of those feelings through lyrics and music can be healing. Just doing the act of writing can be what makes our art valuable.

Other times, we write to communicate our feelings to others. Simply expressing our feelings isn't enough, and we feel the desire to be understood by others and connect with them. When the listener understands our feelings and feels those same feelings as a result of hearing our song, we as the artist feel fulfilled. In this case, what makes our art feel valuable is a notable response from our listener.

Writing song lyrics that people understand and really connect with can be very difficult. There isn't space in a lyric to write paragraphs of description, and so we have to figure out how to tell a story using very few words. Songs try to capture big feelings, such as feeling deceived, lonely, or loved. The same intensity that makes these feelings seem song-worthy also makes them hard to describe accurately. Other times, we aren't clear exactly how we feel or what we have to say that is interesting to the listener. We sometimes compare our own lyrics to the lyrics of our favorite artists, and our own words never seem quite good enough. On top of all that, we often desire to rhyme and fit our words seamlessly to the melody and its rhythms.

The great news about lyric writing is that with a few techniques, you can begin to write faster and connect with your listeners more strongly. With daily practice, you'll gain some confidence and be able to decide for yourself when your lyric is expressing artfully what you want to create.

POINT, POINT, POINT TO YOUR POINT

It may seem obvious that to write a lyric, you need to know what you want to say. But making sure the listener knows what we want to say is even more important. There is one tool that is integral in making sure the listener knows our main message, and that is repetition. Take a moment to sing the lyrics of some of your favorite songs. Can you hear the repetition? Just as repetition of a bit of melody helps us to remember the melody and hear it as uniquely that song, repetition of a lyric line helps us to remember it and understand it as the main idea. A simple tool, repetition is very effective in showing the listener what is the main message of the song.

ACTIVITY 7.1. LYRIC REPETITION

Print out the lyrics of ten songs you enjoy. Highlight any lines of the lyric that are repeated throughout the song. Is the repeated line also the title of the song? In what section does most of the repetition happen? Why do you think repetition happens most in the choruses of most songs?

ACTIVITY 7.2. USING LYRIC REPETITION

A great exercise to practice using repetition is to write a very simple chorus section. Think of a lyric line that you like and use it as a title. Let that be line one of the chorus. The most simple chorus structure repeats the title line four times.

Rumor has it

rumor has it

rumor has it

rumor has it

Try this technique two more times using two other titles. Read them each out loud and feel how the message of the choruses are focused. There is no question what the song is trying to say when only one line is repeated.

Next, try writing a chorus with two different lines. Alternate the lines, like this:

Falling in the deep

waiting for a sign

Falling in the deep

waiting for a sign

Now, the chorus is split between these two ideas, but still focused. We may feel unsure which idea is most important, but the variation may also add interest to the song. A big part of creativity is deciding for yourself when specific tools create a stronger effect, and when they simply just create a different effect. Each song we write presents a new situation in which we can play with the tools of the craft. To use repetition, we've got to have a lyric line that is worth repeating. So how do we come up with ideas, and how do we turn those ideas into song lyrics?

WHAT DO YOU WANT TO SAY?

If you're walking, talking, and breathing, you've got something to say. You might not believe it yet, but the way you see the world around you is unique to who you are. Who you were born to be and the experiences you've had combine to create the richness of who you are, right now at this moment. There are two parts to writing lyrics that are fulfilling to both the writer writing them and to the listener listening to them.

First, we as writers need to learn to *hear* or sense what matters to us so that we can write our thoughts and feelings down. Writing our thoughts and feelings freely is what we do when we feel inspired. Through some special writing exercises, we can also learn to invite inspiration when we don't feel particularly inspired.

Second, we need to be able to communicate those thoughts and feelings in a way others can understand. This part is where the tools of songwriting come into play. We sometimes need to step outside the song and look at it from the perspective of our listener. That's what it means to be the *observer*. In this chapter, I'll give you several tools for becoming the observer so that when you write, you can feel and be better understood.

JOURNALING AND SENSORY WRITING

Lyrics differ from storytelling or poetry in that they are tethered by song form and distinct and repeating rhythms and rhyme schemes. Sometimes, these rhythms and rhyme schemes just fall out onto the page, and we don't need to do any editing. But most of the time, inspiration doesn't carry us through the writing of the whole lyric. Many times, the inspiration doesn't give us much more than the initial idea.

The first step in getting an idea onto the page is to do what is called *sensory writing*. It's a lot like journaling, but instead of writing about our feelings, we write about our feelings through our senses of taste, touch, sight, sound, smell, and movement. When we write with our senses, we paint a picture for the listener. So instead of *telling* the listener how we feel, we *show* them. That means the listener is "living" the experience, rather than simply watching us as the singer tell about our experiences. Let's look at a few sensory writings from some beginning writers to understand what "showing" rather than "telling" looks like.

Sensory Writing on "Hospital Room," by Maya Cook, 17, Salt Spring Island, BC, Canada:

Long-tired faces are illuminated by fluorescent lighting; inky bags creep under open eyes. The only sound is the static of lights flickering, yet everyone hears the cardiogram beep of their loved ones endlessly, desperately sustaining it so it doesn't fall flat. A woman in an unevenly buttoned white blouse fiddles frantically with a lock of mousey brown hair. Next to me, a little boy sits with a miniature yellow dump truck in his lap, his father's hand clenched on his knee. It smells like crumpled tissues and prescription pills. The white starch of the nurses' shirts set off an eerie glow and the blood red clock stretches and pulls at each second until it snaps. I anxiously pull out the contents of my pockets, only to find ferry tickets and crumbs of blue lint. The air condenses as a nurse walks in, her confined heels heralding her coming. Her painted lips draw every tired eye, each person ready to breathe in her news as they part.

This sensory writing has the power to pull the listener into the hospital room, as if we're watching and experiencing what's going on there. We forget about our own lives for a moment, and it's almost like we're living a movie scene within the set Maya has constructed for us. She's got great adjectives, like "long-tired" and "fluorescent" and "inky," specific verbs like "creep" and "flicker," and she has a talent for noticing small details that would normally seem insignificant to write about. But what Maya really does well here is capture an emotion. The emotion is expressed through the way she experiences the hospital room. It's sad, scary, and looming. The emotion is tension, fear, with the desire to run. Notice how Maya never told us how she feels? She never uses any of those feeling words to express what she wants or needs. Yet, we know. We know because we experience the world of that hospital room as she does, and we begin to feel as she feels.

Let's look at some more sensory writing.

Sensory writing on "Locket" by Phoenix Lazare, 18, from Salt Spring Island, BC, Canada:

> *It was a light shade of auburn, rusty and fragile. The sides wore a golden lining and smelled like an old book. Dim light pours through small cracks in the blinds as the evening lingers in silence, and these walls are no longer ours. A distant reflection in the window catches the familiar locket that lies in the depths of my palm, and I'm glad we tried. The long chain once fell beside my heart and held a worn photo from the night we fell in love. Fingerprints still remain on the aged pendant. Every inch of this place holds a memory.*

In this sensory writing, Phoenix started with an object to write about, a locket. The object brought up lots of great ideas about the significance of a locket, what it meant to her, what memories it held, and even what she's learned about life and love through it. The locket is just a locket until it becomes emotionally significant. To her, the locket wasn't just a piece of metal. It was a part of her life.

Here is another sensory writing example, by Ocea Goddard, 17, from Salt Spring Island, BC, Canada. Notice how Ocea describes the situation. Instead of telling us how she feels, she describes "crossing his arms" and "grabbing onto the hem of my dress." These are just two descriptions that show us how she perceives and feels this important moment in her life.

> *Three seconds longer than I'd liked. My palms start to sweat as I fidget my feet out of force of habit. Digging the fraying edges into the sparse gravel. Lightly shifting my weight side to side. Mouth dry, I try to speak, but it comes out in croaked mumbles. Crossing his arms, he looks away, unimpressed. The buzz of summer cicadas and gusts of passing cars fill the void but still it feels like forever. Grabbing onto the hem of my dress for comfort, I rub the cotton between my fingers, still raw from yesterday's playing. He looks up, and I can see the ghost of the comfort once on his face and the cold acceptance it holds now.*

So, how do we write with our senses, and how do we turn that into song lyrics?

I'll show you a few tools for that, and as you become more comfortable with them, you'll come up with some tools for yourself too.

CAPTURE THE MOMENT

The most important idea in writing interesting and sense-bound language is to try to capture a single moment rather than a broad stretch of time. Instead of trying to tell lots of story, focus on trying to describe in detail a pivotal and powerful single moment. Imagine you had sixty seconds to tell the story of something really important that happened to you. Maybe it was the day your family moved, maybe it was starting a new relationship with someone, maybe it was ending one. In sixty seconds, you'd need to summarize a lot of the story. There wouldn't be time to accurately describe how you felt, and the intensity of the situation. Now, imagine I gave you five minutes to talk about that same event. You'd be able to go into detail, taking me through the significant moments that left you feeling sad, excited, heartbroken, or hopeful. In songs, we don't have a long time to make the listener believe our moment was powerful. But we do have the power of our senses to snap a picture of the most important moment, and recreate it for the listener so they can see it, hear it, touch it, taste it, smell it, and experience it for themselves.

DON'T JUST WALK: SAUNTER, HOBBLE, OR GLIDE

You are the photographer of your life, and your goal is to show people what matters so they can feel how much it matters too. Let's go back to Maya's sensory writing and look at how she is able to show how significant this moment of life really is.

> Long-tired faces are **illuminated** by fluorescent lighting; inky bags **creep** under open eyes. The only sound is the static of lights **flickering**, yet everyone hears the cardiogram beep of their loved ones endlessly, desperately **sustaining** it so it doesn't **fall** flat. A woman in an unevenly buttoned white blouse **fiddles** frantically with a lock of mousey brown hair. Next to me, a little boy **sits** with a miniature yellow dump truck in his lap, his father's hand **clenched** on his knee. It smells like crumpled tissues and prescription pills. The white starch of the nurses' shirts **set off** an eerie glow and the blood red clock **stretches** and **pulls** at each second until it **snaps**. I anxiously **pull** out the contents of my pockets, only to **find** ferry tickets and crumbs of blue lint. The air **condenses** as a nurse **walks** in, her confined heels **heralding** her coming. Her painted lips **draw** every tired eye, each person ready to **breathe in** her news as they **part**.

Let me say that as a high school student, I was never very interested in English grammar. If you are, you'll find this detailed look at language more fun than I did. But if the idea of trying to identify verbs, nouns, and adjectives scares you, stick with me just a little longer. You won't need to become an expert at grammar to write great sensory language.

The words that are in bold are verbs. The verbs show action, movement. The action words of our writing are the most powerful words in bringing the moment we're describing to life. Notice how these action words are specific in many cases. Instead of "lighted," Maya says "illuminated." Instead of "move," Maya says "creep," "stretches," and "drew." Some of the verbs are still general, such as "walk" and "sit." We don't need to get specific with every single verb, but the more we do get specific, the more emotion is expressed. Verbs show motion, and motion shows emotion. When I "fiddle" with a button, I'm frustrated. I feel upset, or distracted, or maybe angry. If I simply "unbutton" the button, there is no sense for how I felt as I did it. When we write using sensory language, we are simply describing the picture we see in our mind. The things that we see are what make our writing unique and what show the listener the way we feel. Notice how all the details that Maya noticed in her hospital writing carried the same basic emotion? All the details point to feeling alone and scared. Verbs have an incredible power to show how we're feeling without us having to say it.

ACTIVITY 7.3. USING SPECIFIC VERBS

Practice getting specific with verbs. To do this, get your hands on a thesaurus, either a physical copy or online. A thesaurus gives us *synonyms*—words that mean roughly the same thing as other words. Take a few minutes to look up a verb such as "move" or "shake" or "roll" or "flow" in a thesaurus. At first, you might use the thesaurus frequently to come up with more specific verbs, but you'll find that with practice, the verbs that accurately express how you feel come more quickly as you write.

ADJECTIVES AND NOUNS, METAPHORICALLY SPEAKING

Two other important parts to our language are the nouns and adjectives. Nouns are those person, place, animal, or thing words. Adjectives usually come before the noun, describing it. Sometimes, adjectives do a great job showing us emotion, but many times, they just show us the facts. The dump truck was yellow, so it's a "yellow dump truck." The tissues were crumpled, so they're "crumpled tissues." But many times, adjectives are interesting because they create what we call a "metaphor" with the noun. A *metaphor* is when we see something as something else. "Painted lips" is a metaphor, because we're seeing lips as if they were painted. Of course, lips aren't painted, but just colored with lipstick. To practice grabbing more interesting adjectives, try the following two simple exercises.

ACTIVITY 7.4. USING IMAGES TO GET SPECIFIC

Open up a magazine or book to a picture that intrigues you. Begin describing what you see. Try to get as specific as you can. If you see sky, describe the sky. If you see nature, describe it in terms of how you think it would feel to touch it and smell it. If you see faces, are they wrinkled or young? Is the scene bustling or peaceful? If the picture brings a memory of your own to mind, follow that and describe the memory in detail. Whenever you use a person, place, animal, or thing word, describe it with an adjective. If the adjective seems more general, try getting more specific.

ACTIVITY 7.5. METAPHORICAL COLLISSIONS

A great way to come up with interesting metaphors is to make an arbitrary list of five adjectives and five nouns. Try "colliding" one of the nouns against each of the five adjectives. Write down any of the combinations that sound interesting to you. Then try colliding another noun with each of the five adjectives.

Adjectives	Nouns
crunchy	paper
salty	popcorn
soft	words
fast	conversation
tired	hands

crunchy paper
crunchy popcorn
crunchy words
crunchy conversation
crunchy hands

Notice how the adjectives and nouns that are not normally expected to be heard together create interesting collisions. The adjectives that are expected to be heard with the nouns don't create any metaphor at all, but they may still create a good specific description. Crunchy popcorn is just crunchy popcorn, but crunchy conversation is an interesting way to describe a conversation that might be argumentative, or perhaps spiked with interesting gossip. When we allow ourselves to see one thing as another, we are using metaphor. The more specific instead of general we can be, the stronger our metaphors can become.

ACTIVITY 7.6. 10 MINUTES A DAY

Learning to describe moments of your life with sensory language can seem difficult, but it's a skill you'll develop quickly if you devote just a little time each day to practicing it. Take ten minutes in the morning right when you wake up, or find some quiet time before you go to bed, and grab your phone or laptop and start typing. You might prefer a pencil and paper, or, you might prefer to talk your sensory writing out loud into a recorder. Any way you do it is okay. What matters most is how comfortable you feel as you do it.

To get started, choose an object or a place to write about. Write the sensory words "taste, touch, sight, sound, smell, and movement" at the top of the page. Don't think too much before you start writing, but just let the words flow. If your mind seems to go blank, remind yourself of the sensory words at the top of the page.

FLAUNT WHAT YOU'VE GOT

Ten minutes a day of sensory writing can certainly help us to describe ideas in more detail. But, sensory writing has another great result too. We can actually use the paragraphs of sensory writing we do as actual lines of lyric. When we can really let loose and totally describe how we think and feel and see the world in our sensory writing, our lyric will do that too. But lyric differs from paragraph writing in important ways. Lyric has a rhythm to the lines and a rhyme scheme too. So, how do we take our lines from the ten-minute daily writing and make them into lyric?

LIFTING LINES AND MAKING RHYMES

Rhyme Schemes

A lyric section such as a verse usually has some rhyme. The pattern of rhyme is called the "rhyme scheme." There are some very typical rhyme schemes used in most songs we hear. Knowing these rhyme schemes helps us to write sections that are just as powerful as our favorite songs' verses, prechoruses, choruses, and bridges.

Many sections of our favorite songs are an even number of lines. In other words, we've got two, four, or six lines. Within the section, or at the end of the section, we usually hear a rhyme. Some of the most common rhyme schemes are:

(Read across)

ABAB

XAXA

AABB

AAAA

Matching letters indicate that the two lines rhyme. An "X" means that the line doesn't rhyme with any other line.

For six-line sections, some common rhyme schemes are:

XXAXXA

XABXAB

XAAXBB

ABCABC

Whatever the rhyme scheme we choose, the placement of the rhymed words is what creates what we call closure. *Closure* is what tells the listener's ear that the thought is finished and the section is done. Think of rhyme like a period at the end of a sentence. It tells our ears that we've finished one idea and are about to move on to another.

RHYME GROUPIES

In kindergarten, you learned that "cat" and "hat" rhyme. This is called a "perfect" rhyme. The vowel sound "a" and the ending consonant sound "t" are the same. But there are four other rhyme types that are available to us when we write lyrics. They are:

1. Family Rhyme
2. Additive/Subtractive Rhyme
3. Assonance Rhyme
4. Consonance Rhyme

Family rhyme is when ending consonants are only similar. An example is "cat" and "mad," or "dock" and "lot."

Additive rhyme is when we add a sound or a syllable to the second word of the rhyme pair. An example is "cat" and "hats," or "bold" and "folded."

Subtractive rhyme is when we take away a sound or syllable from the second word of the rhyme pair. An example is "hats" and "cat," or "bead" and "free."

Assonance rhyme is when the ending consonant sound is completely different. An example is "cat" and "man," or "lost" and "wrong."

Consonance rhyme is when the ending consonants match but the vowel sounds do not. This is the only rhyme type where the vowel sounds don't match. An example is: "cat" and "boat," or "need" and "load."

**For a more comprehensive explanation of rhyme, I suggest Pat Pattison's *Songwriting: Essential Guide to Rhyming* (2nd Ed., Berklee Press, 2014).

One important idea with rhyme is that we only hear a rhyme between the emphasized or "stressed" syllables of the words. In other words, "locket" and "forget" don't rhyme because "locket" has the stress on "lock-," but "forget" has the stress on "-get."

A second important idea with rhyme is that the two words must begin with different consonant sounds. "Cat" and "can" aren't rhymes because our ears will be drawn to the similar "c" sound and hear it as repetition rather than as rhyme.

If the different rhyme types seem confusing, try just focusing on the first four types where the vowel sounds are the same. As long as you use words that have the same vowel sound for your rhymes, you'll be working with one of the first four types of rhyme.

BEYOND PERFECT RHYME

You might notice how perfect rhyme limits your options of "what" you write. After all, we might think of a limited list of words rhyming with "sky" such as "high," "try," "goodbye," "deny," "cry," etc. But if you try some of the other rhyme types, you'll find more possibilities such as "tonight," "ride," "sign," or even "higher."

THE RHYMING DICTIONARY

Rhyming dictionaries can be a great way to find more words to use in our lyric. But, when we use the rhyming dictionary, we often only find perfect rhyme. Instead, you can use your rhyming dictionary to come up with other types of rhyme, too, by following this process:

Think of a word that rhymes perfectly with "cat."

Change the ending consonant sound to a related consonant sound to get a family rhyme. To do this, you can exchange the t for a d, g, k, b, or p. An m can be switched out for n, and sh can be switched out for ss or z sounds.

- cat becomes lab, sad, lag, sack, or tap

- lane becomes fame

- fish becomes kiss or biz

Now, look up the new word in the rhyming dictionary. You'll find a list of words that are perfect rhymes for the new word. All those words are rhymes with your original word, just not perfect rhymes. They might be family or assonance rhymes.

Let's go back now to our sensory writing paragraphs. I'm going to show you just how many rhymes are already there, without the writer having even tried to rhyme.

> It was a _light shade_ of auburn, rusty and _fragile_. The _sides_ wore a _golden lining_ and _smelled_ like an _old_ book. _Dim light_ pours through _small cracks_ in the _blinds_ as the evening lingers in _silence_, and these _walls_ are no longer ours. A _distant_ reflection in the window catches the familiar locket that _lays_ in the _depths_ of my _palm_ and I'm glad we _tried_. The long _chain_ once _fell_ beside my heart and _held_ a worn _photo_ from the _night_ we _fell_ in love. _Fingerprints_ still _remain_ on the _aged pendant_. Every _inch_ of this _place holds_ a memory.

To find rhymes, I'm going to look for vowel sounds that match. That way I know I'll have one of those first four types, either perfect rhyme, family rhyme, additive/subtractive rhyme, or assonance rhyme.

light: sides, blinds, silence, tried, beside, night

shade: chain, remain, aged, place, lays

old: golden, holds, photo

fragile: cracks

small: walls, palm

smelled: held, fell

depths: pendant

dim: inch, fingerprints

There are also some weaker rhymes, including some consonance rhyme. Remember that consonance rhyme is when the ending consonant sounds are all that match:

lingers: ours, longer

small: fell

catches: reflection

In just a moment, I'll show you how you can use these rhyme pairs to write the section of lyric from the sensory writing paragraph. But first, let's talk about another important element of lyric writing: rhythm.

GET YOUR LYRIC GROOVE ON

Even before we write music, we can write a lyric that has a rhyme scheme and rhythmic pattern. This will make it easier to set the lyric to music, and we'll more likely be happier with the result when we do. If you've ever read *The Cat in the Hat* or sung nursery rhymes such as "Mary Had a Little Lamb," you've heard how the words have a rhythmic pattern. The rhythmic pattern tells our ears when to expect the rhyme to fall. Try reading this section of three lines out loud. Think about what you expect to hear if there were a fourth line:

Summer sun and backyard pools

teach what we don't learn in school

how to love and be a friend

Each of these lines follows the same rhythmic pattern. The rhyme scheme so far is AAB. The first two lines sets up the expectation for two more lines that follow the same rhythm and rhyme scheme. So, we might expect something like this to finish the section:

Summer sun and backyard pools

teach what we don't learn in school

how to love and be a friend

till autumn falls around again

Now the section feels complete. When you write your lyric, try to feel the rhythm of the words and lines. Saying the lyric out loud can help in hearing the rhythms. Also, keeping the lines short can keep the rhythms much more manageable. Long lines of lyric are difficult to match rhythmically, since the rhythms can become quite haphazard. Now, sometimes we want to give the listener something unexpected, making the rhyme fall in a different position than they thought it would. This is a great way to add interest to the lyric.

EXPECTATION OF RHYME

Just remember: we can't make the rhythm feel unexpected if we don't first give the listener an expectation for repetition.

So, let's try giving the listener a short line in the last line, after three lines that are the same length and rhythm:

Summer sun and backyard pools

teach what we don't learn in school

how to love and be a friend

till the end

This last line is shorter than we might expect, and that creates some great spotlight on that line. It can also lead to an interesting musical area, since our melody would also do something different than expected there too.

Let's go back again to our sensory writing from Phoenix. I'm going to make a few verses from her writing, all fitting into four- or even a five-line section.

Journaling:

It was a light shade of auburn, rusty and fragile. The sides wore a golden lining and smelled like an old book. Dim light pours through small cracks in the blinds as the evening lingers in silence, and these walls are no longer ours. A distant reflection in the window catches the familiar locket that lays in the depths of my palm and I'm glad we tried. The long chain once fell beside my heart and held a worn photo from the night we fell in love. Fingerprints still remain on the aged pendant. Every inch of this place holds a memory.

Verse Option 1:

I held the locket in my palm
as a dim light poured through the blinds
the chain once fell beside my heart
but the sides were still golden lined

Verse Option 2:

I held the locket in my palm
as a dim light poured through the blinds
I caught a distant reflection in the window
and I was glad we tried

Verse Option 3:

I held the locket in my palm
as a dim light poured through the blinds
the chain once fell beside my heart
we fell in love that night

Verse Option 4:

I held the locket in my palm
fingerprints still remained
from the night we fell in love
the memories a rusted chain

Verse Option 5:

Rusted with a fragile chain
fingerprints that still remained
a photo worn and held inside
we fell in love that night

Verse Option 6:

A pendant with a photograph
lingering in silence
the dim light pouring through the cracks
the sides a golden lining
fragile as the evening

Verse Option 7:

Dim light pours in
through cracks in the blinds
the walls are no longer ours
evening lingers in the silence

All these sections result from simply lifting lines from the sensory writing and stacking them to make a lyric. The lines are short, so the rhythms are easier to manage. The rhyme schemes are typical of many of the schemes we hear in our favorite songs. When we construct song lyrics this way, we often end up with a verse section that matches what we really wanted to say. We also make lyric writing easier, because we use the exact lines we already came up with in the journaling while we weren't even trying to write lyric at all.

ACTIVITY 7.7. LIFTING LINES

Try lifting lines from your sensory writing paragraphs. You might try fitting them into four- and six-line sections using the rhyme schemes below, or you might try other rhyme schemes you think of as you go along. It's also okay to add new lines to the sections of lyric as you think of them, even if they weren't in your original sensory writing paragraph.

Typical Rhyme Schemes for Four-Line Sections	ABAB
	AABB
	XAXA
	AABA
	AAAA
Typical Rhyme Schemes for Six-Line Sections	XXAXXA
	XAAXAA
	XAAXBB
	XABXAB
	AABCCB

ACTIVITY 7.8. LOOKING FOR SENSORY LANGUAGE

Take a listen to five of your favorite songs. See if you can identify the sensory language in the verses. Look for lines that have taste, touch, sight, sound, smell, and movement in them. Then, map out the rhyme schemes used for the verses. Do you notice any of our typical patterns?

AWESOME CHORUSES

You already know that the chorus of the song delivers the main message. A chorus tells the listener why the song is significant to the singer, and what the singer wants the listener to walk away knowing. Sometimes, we know just what we want the listener to know. If so, we probably have the title of the song already in mind. Song titles are typically drawn from the chorus, though they don't have to be. They can come from other areas of the lyric, and when they are, they are often chosen because they use interesting language.

In the following pages, I'll show you how I like to arrive at titles and chorus material organically. In other words, when I don't have a clear idea what the song is about, I like to do more journaling to figure it out. Journaling just lets me pour my feelings out onto the page, and the language that comes out often surprises me. It's often a better expression of how I feel, rather than when I sit down with the intent to write great lyric. Let's look at an example of chorus journaling from Phoenix. She did this journaling from the same idea, "locket," as her sensory writing piece. You can do the same, starting a new journal where you left off your original journal.

> *Dust sits atop the rusty metal, reminding me of every precious moment I took for granted. If I could bring you back, I would. If I could scream all of the words I should have said through the clouds and into your ears, I would. If I could build you a house and put all of my love in it, I would. Gentle phrases spilling out of the cracks in the wooden panels, whispering sweet nothings. I miss you. It's been a long time, so long that I can't count the months on my fingers anymore. The pit in my stomach won't go away, and it seems as though all that is left of you is this rusty reminder of what used to be.*

Because the chorus delivers the main message, the language of the chorus is different than the language of the verse. The verse used our senses to describe a moment in time or a specific situation or event. The chorus needs to summarize the meaning of the situation or event so the listener knows what bigger message we're trying to say. So that means that for choruses, we don't hear much sensory language. Instead, we hear big, sprawling ideas that seem to generalize. Sometimes, they may even seem cliché.

Now, let's look at how we can take lines from Phoenix's new journaling and construct a chorus. The first step might be to comb through the writing and look for cool ideas. These might be words or phrases that simply catch our eye. It may be something that simply feels like it really captures what we were trying to say as we wrote it.

> *Dust sits atop the rusty metal, reminding me of every precious moment I took for granted. If I could bring you back, I would. If I could scream all of the words I should have said through the clouds and into your ears, I would. If I could build you a house and put all of my love in it, I would.* **Gentle phrases spilling out of the cracks in the wooden panels,** *whispering sweet nothings. I miss you. It's been a long time, so long that I can't count the months on my fingers anymore.* **The pit in my stomach won't go away and it seems as though** *all that is left of you is this rusty reminder of what used to be.*

Some of these phrases or single words might be great titles. We can choose one to be our title, just by putting it in a powerful position in the chorus and repeating it. We can also take some of those other cool phrases and stack them around the title for a full chorus section. How we stack the lines depends on what we like.

Here are some examples of choruses drawn from Phoenix's journaling:

Chorus Option 1:

It's been a long time
I took you for granted
I miss you
I miss you

Chorus Option 2:

All that's left is this rusty reminder
of what used to be
All that's left is this rusty reminder
of you and me
and I miss you

Chorus Option 3:

I took for granted
every precious moment
I miss you
I miss you
If I could build you a house
and put our love in it
I would
I would

Chorus Option 4:

If I could scream all the words I should have said
and it reached your ears from the clouds
I would, I would
If I could build you a house and fill it with my love
gentle phrases spilling out
I would, I would

BEING THE CENTER OF ATTENTION

Many songs we hear follow familiar chorus structures. These structures often involve repetition of the title in a position called the *hook* or *power position*. This position in the lyric gets a lot of attention, just because of where it is. Repetition and good use of the power position helps the listener be sure what the main message is. It also shows the listener that we as the artist know what we're trying to say! There are a few power positions in a song. The power positions in the chorus are often the first line, the last line, and sometimes the middle line. We might use just one for the title, or all of them to get our message across clearly.

Here are some typical structures for choruses with the power position used to highlight the title, "Falling Fast."

Exact Repetition:

Falling Fast

Falling Fast

Falling Fast

Falling Fast

Internal repetition is a useful tool of taking a portion of a lyric line and repeating it.

Internal Repetition: 4-Line Section

I'm Falling

Falling Fast

I'm Falling

Falling Fast

Internal Repetition: 6-Line Section

Nobody and no one
can ever slow me down
I'm falling fast   *(power position)*
Nobody and no one
can ever slow me down
I'm falling fast   *(power position)*

Immediate repetition of the title in a longer "falling fast" section works well.

Internal Repetition: Longer Section

Falling fast
I'm falling fast
and no one can slow me down
I'm falling fast
falling fast
one day I might hit the ground
but I'm having too much fun for now
falling fast

When we map out the structure of a chorus section, we use "D" to represent "developmental lines," and "T" to represent the title line. Some great chorus structures include TDTD, DTDT, DDTDDT, and TTDTTD.

We can also add the title line at the end of any of these structures, making a section of an odd number of lines. When we do this, the message of the song is even clearer. It's the last idea the listener hears, and often the idea that is repeated most.

Note that "T" and "D" don't refer to rhyme scheme, but only whether the line is the title line or a line that just delivers other important chorus ideas.

ACTIVITY 7.9. MAPPING THE RHYME SCHEME

Listen to the chorus of five of your favorite songs. Try mapping out the chorus sections, noticing the rhyme scheme and the position of the title in those power positions. Notice that choruses may not use much rhyme at all, particularly when there is lots of repetition of the title. See if you find any structures you like and can use as a map for your own choruses.

ACTIVITY 7.10. LIFTING AND STACKING CHORUSES

A fun exercise is to write only choruses for a whole week. Try taking a line from a journaling exercise you've done, or choosing a title from your idea book. Try developing a few different choruses from that single title, first by journaling around that title idea and then stacking your favorite lines from the paragraph into chorus sections. Try using the different structures we discussed here and any others you like from your own listening examples.

BEAM ME UP, SCOTTY: BRIDGES AND PRECHORUSES

Two other common sections we'll find in songs are bridges and prechoruses. The prechorus follows the verse preceding the chorus. The musical function of a prechorus is often to create some suspense, winding us up before the chorus comes and relieves all that expectation. Lyrically, prechoruses tend to do the same thing. Instead of telling us the big message like the chorus does, prechoruses often ramp us up to want to hear the main message of the chorus. Sometimes, this means the prechorus lyric tells more about the verse story, asks questions, or just gives us one final thought that prepares us for the title. You might find prechorus material in your sensory writing, or, you may find it in your chorus journaling. Just be careful not to give the main message away in your prechorus section, or it will deflate the chorus message. In other words, if a song is like a good joke, don't tell the punch line halfway through the joke. Wait until the end of the joke, the chorus, to hit us with the punch.

Bridges are sometimes easier to hear than prechoruses, because musically, their function is to take our ears somewhere new. It may be a new groove, a very different melody, or even a new key. Lyrically, bridges function the same way. Instead of recapping the verse or chorus ideas, we often tell the listener what we're going to do now, how things will be different in the future, or the big lesson that we've learned that we want the listener to understand. If our song is about another person, we might use the bridge to show how that person transformed, or how the problem that person was dealing with has resolved. I like to ask myself this question to think of what to write for the bridge: "Now that I know what I know, what now?" By asking myself this, the bridge considers what the future will be like, or what the moral of the story is. Your bridges may be as simple as one line repeated a few times, or a longer section that tells more story. You might get your bridge ideas from your sensory journaling, or your chorus journaling.

Let's try using some of Phoenix's ideas to use as a prechorus and bridge. There are many options, but from the great ideas she has in her writing, here are a few possibilities:

> *Dust sits atop the rusty metal, reminding me of every precious moment I took for granted. If I could bring you back, I would. If I could scream all of the words I should have said through the clouds and into your ears, I would. If I could build you a house and put all of my love in it, I would.* **Gentle phrases spilling out of the cracks in the wooden panels,** *whispering sweet nothings. I miss you. It's been a long time, so long that I can't count the months on my fingers anymore.* **The pit in my stomach won't go away and it seems as though** *all that is left of you is this rusty reminder of what used to be.*

Prechorus Option 1:

> *I took for granted every precious moment*
> *the feeling won't go away*

Prechorus Option 2:

> *Dust on rusty metal*
> *reminding me*
> *of every precious moment*
> *every precious moment*

Prechorus Option 3:

Dust on metal
this rusty reminder
of what used to be
whispering sweet nothings
whispering sweet nothings

Bridge Option 1:

I can't count the months on my fingers
It's been such a long time
I miss you and all I want to find....

Bridge Option 2:

Gentle phrases spilling out
of cracks in wooden panels
If I could I'd bring you back
I'd bring you back
I'd bring you back

Bridge Option 3:

All the words I should have said
all the love I didn't give
Just dust on top of rusted metal
I miss you
I miss you

Now, I'll choose the ones I like that fit nicely together:

Verse:

I held the locket in my palm
as a dim light poured through the blinds
the chain once fell beside my heart
but the sides are still golden lined

Prechorus:

Dust on rusty metal
reminding me
of every precious moment
every precious moment

Chorus:

If I could scream all the words I should have said
and it reached your ears from the clouds
I would, I would
If I could build you a house and fill it with my love
gentle phrases spilling out
I would, I would

Bridge:

I can't count the months on my fingers
It's been such a long time
I miss you oh if I....

Chorus:

...Could scream all the words I should have said
and it reached your ears from the clouds
I would, I would
If I could build you a house and fill it with my love
gentle phrases spilling out
I would, I would

The bridge of a song typically flows right back into a last chorus. Here, I've made the last words of the bridge "if I" flow back into the chorus "…could scream."

This song lyric came from just a few short paragraphs of journaling. The original journal had some great sensory language, and that made verse writing easier to do. The second journal had honest and beautiful language that supplied the chorus lyric. From the two journals, we got a good prechorus and bridge. It doesn't take much material sometimes to come up with a good lyric. What is more important than lots of ideas is an eye for how to organize those ideas into a song structure. With your knowledge of what kind of language belongs in a verse, chorus, and even bridge and prechorus, you'll be able to write more powerful songs, more quickly, and be more attuned to what you really want to say.

VERSE/REFRAIN SONGS WITH SENSORY WRITING

We can use a similar process that we use for verse/chorus songs to write verse/refrain songs. Instead of writing a chorus, we'll need to choose our title and use it in the last line position of the verse, or the refrain position. Verse/refrain songs sometimes just look like three long verses, with the refrain at the end of each longer verse, and a bridge between the second and third verse/refrain.

Verse/Refrain	Verse/Refrain	Bridge	Verse/Refrain

I'm going to use journaling from Maya Cook to come up with a verse/refrain section. I'll also draw from her more feeling-oriented second journaling she did for chorus material to get second verse and bridge ideas.

Here is Maya's original journaling:

*Long-tired faces are illuminated by fluorescent lighting;
inky bags creep under open eyes. The only sound is the static
of lights flickering, yet everyone hears the cardiogram beep
of their loved ones endlessly, desperately sustaining it so it
doesn't fall flat. A woman in an unevenly buttoned white
blouse fiddles frantically with a lock of mousey brown hair.
Next to me a little boy sits with a miniature yellow dump
truck in his lap, his father's hand clenched on his knee. It
smells like crumpled tissues and prescription pills. The white
starch of the nurses" shirts set off an eerie glow and the blood
red clock stretches and pulls at each second until it snaps. I
anxiously pull out the contents of my pockets, only to find
ferry tickets and crumbs of blue lint. The air condenses as
a nurse walks in, her confined heels heralding her coming.
Her painted lips draw every tired eye, each person ready to
breathe in her news as they part.*

Maya's new, feeling-oriented journaling:

*My tears are coals. They burn the creases of my eyes and feed
off the light. In fact, my whole body is beset by coals. Each
breath heats up as it creeps down my windpipe and bursts,
expelling fire in my belly. What if he doesn't make it? All
we've ever had is breathless smiles and empty words, and
the blood red clock eats up the time we have left to fill them.
Everyone in this breathless room is terribly alone. We sit as
soldiers, marching side-by-side and silhouetted from within
on a barren field. No one can accompany death. So we wait,
remembering. Every heart grasps tightfisted onto their hope:
big fish wriggling and gasping until there is only a single,
glimmering, scale left. Everything looks different in the light.*

Verse/Refrain 1:

This place smells like prescription pills
the only sound is the static of the lights
till the nurse walks in in her starched white shirt
her painted lips drawing every tired eye
we sit as soldiers marching side-by-side
in this waiting room grasping tight
to hope that everything will look different
in the light, in the light

Verse/Refrain 2:

I watch the little boy next to me
sitting on his father's lap
as the clock on the wall stretches and pulls
each second until it snaps
I feel the tears burn my eyes
those tears are coals, my body fire
I could only see what the darkness hides
in the light, in the light

Bridge:

All you and I have ever had
were breathless smiles and empty words
breathless smiles and empty words

Verse/Refrain 3:

> *No one can accompany death*
> *I know that it's a barren field*
> *this clock is eating up the time*
> *that we have left to finally heal*
> *now my heart is grasping tight*
> *like a wriggling fish gasping for life*
> *if I get the chance, I'll make it right*
> *in the light, in the light*

I added two lines that were not in the original journals, to connect the ideas with content that summarized rather than added more small detail. It is always okay to add new lyrics, as long as we feel the new lines carry the same mood as the original lyric lines.

Verse/refrain sections you write might be six lines long, or much longer. The bridge might be very short with just two lines, or it might be quite long with six lines or more. The important idea is that each verse is summarized with the refrain line, or "hook." In this song, the refrain was "in the light," which may also be the title of the song. This line shows the listener how each verse is connected—through the idea of "light."

CLEANING UP YOUR ACT

Getting a first draft of our lyric can take time, but particularly if you like to have everything perfect before writing it down. There are some benefits to just scribbling ideas onto the page, without worrying whether they're in perfect shape or not. One of the benefits is that we can write faster, and stay more objective as we do. That means we're more likely to hear how the listener hears our song. Sometimes, we need to take a break from the song after we've written it to get that objective point of view back. Taking a week away from the lyric can be a great way to see problems we couldn't see before.

Here are some great editing tools that can help you clean up a messy lyric, or check to see whether the lyric is as easy to understand for the listener as it is for us, the writers.

WRITE LIKE YOU TALK

When we talk, we use full sentences. We use the same tense as we tell a story, not flipping between past and future. We keep the characters the same, so the pronouns are understood. Let me show how quickly a lyric can get messy when these things aren't clear:

Walking holding hands

she sees he cares

waited for the chance

to take the truth or dare

for you to show you're worth it

me to gather courage

she'll always be there

This lyric is difficult to read, and would be difficult to hear in a song for a few reasons. The lines are one-offs: fragments that never quite make a full sentence. The tense changes from line to line, from "walking" and "holding," which are present tense, to "waited" which is past tense. The pronouns are mixed up, using "she," "he," and "you" and "me," so it's unclear who the song is really about. We can fix all these problems by smoothing out "who" the song is about, "when" the song is happening, and by connecting the lines using prepositions and conjunctions so it reads like a story or conversation you might have with a good friend.

Walking holding hands

seeing that you care

I'm waiting for the chance

to take the truth or dare

and show you that you're worth it

so I'm gathering my courage

to prove to you I'll always be there

A great way to make sure the lyric is conversational is to read it aloud. If you're still unsure, put the lyric away for a week and then take it out again and read it out loud as if you're performing it in a play on stage. If any area felt difficult to read or speak, check it for conversational quality. Check to make sure the pronouns (I, you, he, she, they, us, universal you) are clear, the tense (past, present, future) is consistent, and that you're using full sentences.

WRITE WHAT YOU KNOW

Sometimes, we sit down to write a song, and it seems we can't get the ideas out fast enough. Other times, we sit down to write, and nothing seems to flow at all. Inspiration is unpredictable, but there is one thing that helps it to drift around more often and stay longer: write what you know. If you know about cars, write about them in your songs. If you know about moving around a lot, having friends you can count on, or working really hard to do something great for yourself, your family, or your community, write about that. The more you write about what you feel strongly about, the more powerful your songs will be.

It can be alluring to try to write songs just like our favorite artists, but remember, you are unique, and your songs will be unique too when they carry a reflection of your uniqueness in them. If you want to shine as an artist, open a door that lets your inner feelings and thoughts out, and resist the urge to compare your ideas with those of other artists who may have different thoughts, feelings, and messages.

There is nothing new under the sun, and art is no different. Most art expresses the same messages over and over again. What distinguishes some art from the pack is how it's expressed: and that comes from the unique perspective of the artist him/herself.

CHAPTER 8

Activities for Songwriting Groups and Classes

Here are some ideas to get the creativity of a group flowing. Some of these activities can be done solo, collaboratively, or in groups of two to four, and others involve the whole group.

ACTIVITY 8.1. PHYSICAL SENSORY WRITING

To encourage sensory description, take a fifteen-minute walk alone or with a partner, and describe what you see, hear, taste, touch, smell, and observe moving around you. Listening to what your partner experiences can spark ideas within yourself, and really get the sensory description flowing. Sometimes, the physical movement of walking helps to jump-start our creativity, too.

ACTIVITY 8.2. REFLECTIVE LISTENING WITH SENSORY WRITING

Share a page from your sensory writing journal with a writing partner. Let your partner reflect back to you some of the most interesting language you used. Let them describe to you the emotion they felt, and even what might be the song idea generated from that sensory writing. Then, switch places and you become the listener as your partner reads. Another interesting effect is to read your partner's sensory writing yourself as the author listens. Hearing our own ideas read aloud can shine a different light on the words we choose, and we can sometimes hear ideas we didn't hear when we were the writer or reader.

ACTIVITY 8.3. REFLECTIVE LISTENING FOR VERSES AND CHORUSES

In a group of two or three, share a page from your sensory writing journal. Let your partners observe what language of yours might be good chorus or title material, and what might be good verse material. Pay close attention to whether the writing is particularly sensory or not. Very sensory writing will offer more verse lyric, while less sensory writing will seem better for choruses.

ACTIVITY 8.4. PHOTOS AND WORDS

Gather photographs of interesting places, faces, or objects from sources such as magazines or online images. Make a list of some interesting and random words, and write one each on a small piece of paper. Lay out the words and photographs on the floor in the middle of the songwriting group. Assign pairs or let the songwriters of the group pair themselves, and have them choose a photograph and a word that interests them. The goal of the partnership is to write a song, lyric and music, in no more than an hour, inspired by the photograph and using the word within the lyric. Songwriters can then share their collaborative songs with the larger group, first presenting the photo and the word before playing the song.

ACTIVITY 8.5. CRUMPLED PAPER

Have each songwriter take out a sheet of paper. On the paper, everyone writes something they deeply want to tell someone, but are afraid to. Crumple up the paper, and throw it in the middle of the room. After everyone has contributed a paper ball, have the songwriters each choose a crumpled paper and unfold it. (If any songwriter gets their own writing, have them throw the paper back and choose a different one.) Each songwriter will write a song based on the idea they chose, perhaps even using the language on the paper as the actual chorus section of the song. Have everyone perform their songs next time the group meets.

ACTIVITY 8.6. METAPHOR

Divide the songwriters into three groups. One group will make a list of nouns, another group a list of verbs, and another group a list of adjectives. Have each group write their lists on a common board visible to everyone. Ask students to "collide" a noun with a verb, or a noun with an adjective, or a noun with a noun. Encourage songwriters to form sentences using the collisions that arise from these random pairings.

ACTIVITY 8.7. GUIDED MEDITATION

Turn off the lights, and ask the group to close their eyes. Help the group to quiet down and still their bodies. Encourage them to let their mind drift, being aware of what feelings rise to the surface while they sit in silence. Suggest feelings they may have, such as boredom, frustration, impatience, or eagerness, excitement, and racing thoughts. Continue to let them steep in the moment. Suggest what else might be going through their minds, such as not wanting to be here, or being distracted with things that happened just before coming to the meeting. Ask them to let it go, and enter into the present moment. After some silence, ask them what emotions they feel in their body and where they feel them. Ask them if they feel a tugging, a slight or strong nudging from within that is speaking out. If that feeling were given a voice, what would it be saying? If that feeling were writing a song, what would that song say? Turn the lights up enough for participants to see computer screens or paper, and have them journal for ten minutes.

ACTIVITY 8.8. BEING THE EXPERT

Pair up with another writer. Consider something you are really good at, perhaps even an expert at, and talk about it for five minutes to your partner. Tell any stories that come to mind about how you found the activity or knowledge you're an expert on, and what keeps you doing and pursuing it. Let your partner ask you questions about it too. When you're finished, have your partner reflect back to you your feelings about the activity or knowledge you know so well. See if that matches up with the way you view your own feelings. Together with your partner, talk about how you might build a song out of the feelings and the activity/ knowledge that you hold so dear and know so well.

ACTIVITY 8.9. SPOKEN WORD

Find a short spoken-word performance, not greater than four or five minutes, that inspires you on YouTube. Dim the lights, and play the spoken word piece for the group. After the piece is over and without discussing the performance, let songwriters journal for several minutes about their thoughts and feelings. Using different art forms to inspire our own songwriting is a wonderful way to bring ideas to the surface we didn't know we had.

ACTIVITY 8.10. MELODIC MOTIFS

Play a simple two- or four-chord progression on piano or guitar. Simple works best, so that everyone can easily imagine melodies that may suit the progression. Looping the progression, go around the group and have each songwriter sing an eight-bar melody with the creation of a strong melodic motif in mind. Encourage songwriters to use repetition of this motif throughout the eight bars. Compliment participants on their willingness to sing if they aren't singers, create something without much preparation, and take chances in front of the group. Have songwriters notice the parts of each melody that are catchy or "hooky."

ACTIVITY 8.11. GUIDED FEEDBACK

Before a writer performs a song for the group, hand out a guided feedback sheet to encourage helpful comments. Feel free to use the questions below on your sheet, or add questions that focus on your topics for discussion for the meeting.

Is the message of the song clear? Try reflecting back to the writer(s) what you heard as the main message of the song.

What is the song form? Are the different sections easy to identify?

What really drives this song—melody, lyric, groove, harmonic interest, or performance? Is that the strongest element? How does that element help the song to work?

Can you identify the weakest element of the song—melody, lyric, groove, harmonic interest, or performance? Does this weak element distract you from the strong elements? What suggestions do you have as the listener to strengthen this area of the song?

What qualities in the songwriter's personality can you observe also shine in the songwriter's song? Share this to help the songwriter become aware of when and how her own unique artistry is expressed through her art.

ACTIVITY 8.12. WRITE HAPPY

So often, we write songs using the emotions of sadness, loneliness, and loss. Challenge writers of the group to write a happy song, paying special attention to starting with a groove at a perky tempo. This exercise is nicely done collaboratively or in groups of three.

ACTIVITY 8.13. 40 MINUTES

Writing a song can be great fun, but finishing a song can be miserable. If you find it difficult to finish songs, require weeks or months to write them, or are simply short on time to write, consider this exercise. Each day for three weeks, write a song a day in just forty minutes. The results will force you to grow as a writer. With the seconds ticking in the background, you'll have to submit to less than perfect lyric and music. You'll create an environment in which both dull and sparkling ideas are welcome. Furthermore, you'll generate ideas at a pace that doesn't allow you to look back. After three weeks, you may take more time on some songs, but I encourage you to always have many songs in the works at any given time. This is to ensure that you don't get so hung up on one idea that you live in denial about its frailties. I can look each song in the objective eye and make changes without feeling like it's all I've got going for me. Share the top three of the twenty-one songs you wrote with a partner or group. Talk about any growth you see in your process and results, and hear from others how they perceive you to have grown too.

CHAPTER 9

Next Steps

Not all songwriters play an instrument. But being able to play an instrument even minimally can be very satisfying for the beginning writer. Not only can we begin to reflect what we hear in our head on our instrument, we can experiment with new chords that inspire growth in our songwriting. If you don't play an instrument, picking up some skills on piano or guitar may not be as difficult as you think. Here are some tips on how you might approach building some instrumental skills. Some of my favorite resources related to these topics are listed in appendix C.

GUITAR

Guitar is an instrument that is popular among songwriters. It is easy to transport, and it provides a nice rhythmic foundation for our songs in addition to the harmonic foundation. A decent guitar can be inexpensive, particularly if you find one used.

When you begin learning acoustic guitar, you'll first get a few basic chords under your belt. Once you learn these few chords, you'll soon be able to play a lot of songs from your favorite artists. You'll also learn to strum chords, and even fingerpick depending on the styles of music you wish to play. Playing along with some records in the style you wish to emulate can be a great way to really internalize the groove and be able to express that groove better on your instrument.

I picked up guitar in college after recognizing that I could create high-energy grooves with various strumming patterns more easily than I could create those same high-energy grooves on piano. After learning just a few chords, I was writing rock and country grooves that expanded my writing style by leaps and bounds.

As with any instrument, it helps to know some basic theory, including the circle of fifths, to understand how chords flow into one another and how they are related. But to start, you'll be encouraged by how just a few weeks of practice give you the opportunity to express yourself with an instrument supporting your melody and lyrics.

Nice alternatives or additions to guitar are ukulele and mandolin. Consider these additional instruments songwriters use to support and grow their writing and performance.

A *capo* is a tool songwriters use to change keys without having to change the fingering of the chords we're playing. Though I don't recommend letting a capo keep you from becoming more proficient on your instrument, do take advantage of this wonderful tool to write and play along with other songs in keys you're not yet familiar with.

PIANO

You might be surprised what you can play after just a few months dedicated to learning piano. I believe anyone can learn at least a few basic skills that allow us to write and accompany ourselves. Before you begin playing in the style you wish to play, you'll need to learn some basics. How to play triads in both hands in a few keys, and bass or root movement in your left are good skills to build on. One of the most important skills to develop involves thoughtful expression of the dynamic build of the song. If you're interested in learning to play contemporary and popular music styles, the approach you use to learn piano will be very different than if you want to play classical.

VOICE

The more you sing out loud as you write, the better a singer you'll become. Combine that steady practice with vocal lessons, and you'll notice definite improvement over the course of just a few months. As with learning another instrument, it's important to find an instructor who understands the style of music you want to sing. There are some basic skills and exercises vocal instructors will offer, involving how the mechanism of the voice produces sound, the importance of breath and support, ear-training, and many more. But great vocal coaches will help you to adopt a technique that gives you greater flexibility, strength, and endurance as a vocalist. Make sure to discuss your vocal goals with your coach, and try to define what and how much you'll need to practice to reach those goals.

TEACH ME YOUR WAYS, OH WISE ONE

If you want to write in different genres, you'll need to become aware of the rhythms and chord voicings that make that genre sound the way it does. Listening and playing along with your favorite songs within the genre is a first step in being able to write in that genre too. Having outside help to really understand the techniques used in playing a particular genre can speed the process along. When you're ready to look for a songwriting teacher, try to clarify first what kinds of music you're most interested in learning to play. Most musicians enjoy music of all kinds, but when it comes to playing, writing, or singing, we find our niche and begin to specialize. Bring a few songs that show the kinds of instrumental skills you'd like to gain in your lessons. Ask the teacher what genres he or she enjoys playing most, and why. It's true that we can learn a lot from a teacher with more experience in any genre, but it may also be true for you that the teacher who is very familiar with the genre you love will have ideas and procedures for teaching that keep you inspired and help you learn faster.

If your options are limited in terms of teachers interested in your genre of music, you might explore taking lessons remotely. For instance, maybe you're a fan of the keyboardist or guitarist in a specific band, so try contacting that person for a few lessons via Skype. The worst that person can tell you is "no," but then he/she may refer you to someone who would like to teach you. If you're a teen, remember to talk with your parents first about contacting anyone online. They can help make sure the interaction is safe and as effective as possible.

Another great resource is colleges and universities in your area. Many have music programs or adult classes of some kind, and it just might be a great place to visit to find a good teacher.

Lastly, try going to a few shows in your local town. If you see an instrumentalist you enjoy, approach them and tell them you're looking for a teacher. They may be open to helping you, or know just the person who is.

HOW MUCH SHOULD I PRACTICE?

When it comes to playing an instrument, what you put in is what you get out. The more time you put towards practicing music that challenges you, the better you'll get.

Thirty minutes a day is a good ballpark for beginners. For the more serious musician, many more hours are needed. If you stay focused and use the time to work on the skills that are difficult for you, you'll see improvement over the course of even just a week. Daily practice is better than taking six days off and spending four hours on your instrument one day. Our fingers and our minds learn by building on skills through repetition.

LISTENING IS PRACTICING

You are what you listen to. As important as practicing our instrument is listening to music that uses our instrument in interesting ways. When we listen, we train our ear to hear what we can later teach our fingers to play. Without listening, our musical instincts don't have the opportunity to sharpen. So, if you want to play pop, listen to pop, but also listen to jazz, blues, and other styles that can influence your instinctual understanding of pop music. As you take in other styles of music, the pop music you express will be influenced by those other styles. This is in part how artists become unique. Instead of simply repeating what has already come before you, you take what has come before and color it with your own interpretation based on all your own influences and experiences. Try listening to a new record every week. Spend some time searching out new artists, particularly going back in time to listen to those artists who influenced the artists you love today.

ROCKING THE BAND

One great way to get better as an instrumentalist and just have fun is to be part of a band. Playing in a band helps us to understand how our instrument is played in context of other instruments. When we play piano with a vocalist, we play differently than when we play solo piano. When we play piano with a bassist, we play differently still. How we approach our instrument depends on what is needed in whatever situation we're in. When we've got band experience, we teach our ears to take in the bigger picture of what is being created.

Getting people together to play isn't hard, but forming a band of musicians whose interests align and who all enjoy working together for hours and hours in the same room can be. Bands can form naturally, as musicians who simply cowrite often or just enjoy hanging out and jamming together. Or, bands can form very intentionally, by a core person or group of people who want to express a focused vision for their songs. Managing the schedules and musical goals of several people in a band is difficult, and much time is spent on logistics such as finding a time and place to rehearse. These things can take away from time spent creating music, and over time, that can become disheartening to any band member. To get some experience playing in a group, finding one other player with whom you enjoy hanging out and creating music can be a good way to start. It could be a friend with whom you pick up an instrument, or it could even be your instructor who plays with you in your lesson each week. It could be someone you hire to rehearse with and play a gig. Starting small helps us to focus on the end goal: producing good music.

Many times, we songwriters want a way to express our songs with a full band sound, and so we're driven to find other players to do just that. It can be an exhilarating experience to hear our songs performed according to how we hear them in our head. But, there is also the tendency to rely on the performance or the arrangement and production that the band brings to make up for a weak song. A duo that really expresses the soul of a song can be much more effective than a five-person band that only recites the notes on the page, never capturing the soul that drives the song in the first place. If you are unable to get together the musicians you long for to express your songs, don't lose heart. Make finding one other musician who can breathe life into the song in a fresh way your goal.

There is no better time than now to decide to start playing an instrument. If you have tried in the past and felt the process of practicing the skills that are hard a grind, then you're in good company. Effective practice isn't fun all the time. Many people stop practicing when the going gets tough, but playing the parts of songs that are easy to play over and over and over again isn't practicing. We're not gaining any skills by playing what comes easily. Great musicianship comes with talent, but also a whole lot of determination and hard, hard work. Determine for yourself how badly you want to be able to play an instrument. Set reasonable short and long-term goals and commit. Share your goals with others to keep yourself accountable. Remember that progress comes in waves, and for long periods we may not see the improvements we're making through practicing until we reach an area of steep growth. Looking back over just three months of dedicated practice, you'll see notable improvement in your skills, and you can be proud that you stuck with it. I've never heard anyone say they regret learning an instrument. The skills you learn through setting the goal and practicing towards it will be with you for life.

SHARING YOUR MUSIC WITH OTHERS

Come out of your shell—and by shell, I mean your living room or basement!

Forming a band is a great way to collaborate with other musicians, but you don't have to form a band to find others to write with. Some great places to meet other writers are in your own community, either at school, or through creative arts groups, drama and theater groups, or creative writing groups. The way songwriters meet their collaborators is usually through referrals from friends or simply hanging out in places where music is played. Good collaborations often arise unexpectedly, and songs can come from just jamming together on our instruments or talking more intentionally about what we want to write. Many people have an interest in writing, whether it be scripts for film and television, Broadway musicals, novels, poetry, or popular music. If you don't know anyone who is interested in writing songs like you are, consider getting together with someone from any of these different backgrounds. The skills they bring to the collaboration can be very different from yours, and could create something unique you may never have written on your own.

When it comes to collaborating, my general rule is that I never collaborate with someone I wouldn't want to hang out with for three hours in a friendly environment. And I always discuss with my collaborator what I'm interested in writing, whether it be the genre or style, or the topics I find interesting. Then, I stay open-minded to my collaborator's desires too. Walking into a collaboration with some good lyric or musical ideas to share is a good start, all the while being flexible to see what your collaborator might have in mind too.

Collaboration is a learned skill. Sometimes, two writers are on a different page from the get-go, and it takes awhile to understand where the other is coming from on an idea. Again, if you enjoy being with the other person, the process of understanding each other can seem enjoyable rather than like work.

Collaboration can happen any way that is comfortable for both of you. It could be via email or video-conferencing, texting, or face to face. It could involve several people or just two. Before a collaborator and I sit down to write, I like to establish my wish that the rights of the song be split equally among writers. Sometimes, I am the one turning ideas into actual lyric or musical bits, and sometimes my collaborator is. Splitting equally reflects the natural shape of the art of songwriting—sometimes the creativity flows, and sometimes it doesn't. And who's to say who the ideas really originated from when two or more people are in the room, all with a common goal.

When collaborators disagree on how to write the song, someone has to give. This can be tricky to navigate, particularly if you're the one giving. I've had situations where an idea of mine turned into something I wasn't proud of with the input of the other writer. Something I've learned to navigate over the years is when to give in to the collaborator's ideas, and when to fight for my own. Each situation is different, and it's important to keep in mind that each song we write is another song we write—not the last and not the best. If I cling to my songs too tightly, I can't see them for what they are—songs that a year later I will see in a more objective light. This is not to say that you should let your cowriter have the last word every time. This is only to say that, sometimes, we fight with blindfolds on. Sometimes, we have to blindly trust a collaborator, who has different skills that sometimes complement our own. We choose collaborators based on a feeling—a sense that they might help us to see possibilities and new angles. If a collaboration doesn't result in a song you love, chalk it up to just one more experience of writing and working with someone else. Sometimes, the song isn't that good, but you had a great time writing it. This can be another reason to continue writing with that person: the very act of writing together feeds your creativity to write more, get more practice, and eventually land on an idea or sound you both think is strong.

FORMING A SONGWRITING GROUP

If you're looking for a group to share songs and be creative with, you might try starting one of your own. Many people are interested in some form of creating, whether it be writing, theater, music, or other art forms. You could begin by advertising at your school or local coffee shop, choosing a monthly meeting spot. Consider involving others to brainstorm how to get the word out about the group. An important part of establishing a group is creating a safe space for people to share that is nonjudgmental. If you're not comfortable leading the group, ask for a volunteer at the first meeting to lead the sharing and discussions. You might start by asking each person to introduce themselves, and talk about what they'd like to get out of a creative group like this. See if anyone has been in a group before, and what they liked and didn't like about it. Group members may be interested in receiving feedback on their art, or may be more interested in just sharing their art for the joy of sharing. Whatever the goal, encourage all members to communicate their expectations for the group, and how they'd like to be involved.

I've found that people are more able to commit to a group if the meetings are kept to a reasonable time, such as an hour and a half. Setting a limit on the number of times the group meets also helps people to commit. People are more likely to commit to meeting six times for twelve weeks rather than indefinitely!

SONGWRITING AS A CAREER

The path to making money with songwriting isn't usually easy to define. There are many opportunities to share our music with others, some paid and some not, and the opportunities that feel right for one writer or artist may feel quite counterintuitive to another. Figuring out what kind of music we write and create, what skills we have to offer, and who needs the music we write, is done over the course of several years, and even over decades.

The industry is constantly changing, but some of the jobs that songwriters do fall into the broader categories below.

Writing for Film and Television

Many artists and bands enjoy small to large paychecks with every portion of a song or full song synced to a film or television show. To get involved in this business, you'll need to research what programs use the kind of music you write. Many times, you'll also need to make a personal connection with the music editor of the film or show. You can find that information in the credits or on the network's website. If you live in a major music city, you may connect personally with people whose job is to find music for film and television, but if you live elsewhere, you may rely on virtual relationships and research to make those connections. Having a Web presence where the editor can easily find out about you as an artist, hear your music, and contact you are key, since editors are extremely busy people with lots of music to choose from. Editors are approached by hundreds, if not thousands, of new artists and writers each year who want their music heard. The name of the game is to be respectful, persistent, and to make it as easy as possible for the editor to use your music for their purposes. Signed acts are generally more expensive to negotiate a deal with than unsigned acts. If you're not signed to a label or publisher, take heart that you can quickly settle on the terms of the agreement, and your terms will likely be cheaper than a major label release. For more information on how to get involved in this side of the industry, you might check out the courses at

Berklee Online, http://online.berklee.edu. You can research this business and many other facets of the music business online as well. Some trustworthy sources include:

- Nashville Songwriters Association International, or NSAI, www.nashvillesongwriters.com
- The American Society of Composers, Authors and Publishers, or ASCAP, www.ascap.com
- Broadcast Music Incorporated, or BMI, www.bmi.com
- Songwriters Guild of America, www.songwritersguild.com

Writing for a Publisher

Publishing companies sign writers to write songs they can pitch to artists who need them. A publisher negotiates a contract with a writer for a term that is usually less than three years, and broken into smaller terms called "options." At the end of each "option," the publisher can decide to take the option and continue working with the writer or to let the writer go. Specific terms depend on the contract, but typically, the publisher retains some or all of the publishing rights for every song the writer writes while signed with the publisher. In return, the publisher pays the writer a draw, which the publisher "recoups" or gets back after the songs begin to make money. Things like the costs of demoing the songs are also figured into the amount the publisher makes back as the songs begin to generate money. A good publishing agreement helps the writer to get songs heard by artists who might want to record them; find opportunities to sync the songs with film, television, and other visual media; and connect with other writers who might want to collaborate. Publishers also take care of administration duties for the songwriter.

Getting a job writing for a publisher starts like any other career in the music industry: with networking. As you meet other musicians in your local or regional area, you'll be building relationships that will eventually open doors to get your music heard. Taking classes, collaborating with whomever you can, going to music venues to watch shows, booking your own shows, and simply getting involved in the music industry are all keys to making opportunities come your way.

Writing for Visual Media

Songs are needed for a variety of situations, including video games and independent films. Writers with the skills to produce their own material in home studios are well equipped to take on these opportunities. Many of these opportunities are found by referrals, and networking within the music industry is key to being considered for these kinds of jobs. The path starts out the same, getting involved in the music scene wherever you are. You never know when you'll meet someone with connections you need. Make sure to do your research, and know who you want to write with or for in your desired industry. Ask specific questions of those people you collaborate with. It may be that they know someone who knows someone, and that referral helps you get one step closer to your goals. If they don't know what you need, they don't know how they can help.

RECORDING ARTIST

Many writers enjoy singing and recording their own material. It's a thrill to be in the studio working on a new record, and the process itself can make all the other hassles of the job worth it. When most people think of being a recording artist, they think of popular bands and artists who are performing and selling their music to hundreds of thousands of fans. They think that the ultimate goal of an artist is to get signed by a record label, and the very act of getting signed assures that the artist will rise to stardom. The assumption is that success of the artist is based almost entirely on the artist's talent. One problem with this assumption is that it is built on an outdated model of the music industry, and only describes the stories of a tiny, tiny fraction of artists out there with a dream and a guitar. As important as good music in the industry today is the willingness to promote our music ourselves, which often means we have to wear a lot of hats. In one week, we write, perform, social network, book gigs, teach, author blogs, write books, event plan, do graphic design, research our market, and chip away at our marketing plan. At the same time, we may hold down a full- or part-time job to cover the costs of living and launching our artist career. Being willing to step into all these roles is part of being a successful recording artist. Most recording artists are unsigned, or signed to small labels, or managed by companies who take care of some of the booking and administrative needs. Recording artists certainly do some recording, but the bulk of the time is spent dedicated to keeping life and work afloat between recordings.

TOURING ARTIST

Some writers tour and make a good living playing other people's songs. We might slip in an original now and then, but the bulk of the draw here is the performance talent of the artist. Corporate events, fundraisers, outdoor concerts, holiday concerts, house concerts, and weddings are some of the ways touring artists make a living. If you like to mingle with people and just love to play regardless of what it is you're playing, and don't mind doing a lot of your own booking and business transactions, this can be very fulfilling work.

BROADWAY AND MUSICALS

Writing for theater is another potential path for those interested and knowledgeable about the craft. Writing for theater requires skills specific to that industry, just as writing country music for the country industry requires much more than just a familiarity with tractors, trucks, and ex-wives. If you truly love the theater, you'll already carry with you a passion for the craft, and that will guide you in gathering the skills you need as you surround yourself with people working in that industry.

Most opportunities don't come to us; we find them through the people we meet. Sometimes, we have to create opportunities to use our craft. For instance, we might suggest to a friend we'll perform at their outdoor party, and from that experience, we might meet someone at the party who is interested in having us play another event they are involved in. We might go to our local bookstore and see that an author is speaking on their book about social justice. If our songs speak a similar message, we might approach the store with the idea of performing just before or after the engagement to draw more people and encourage a more memorable experience. As artists, we're always thinking of opportunities to get our music in front of the people who will appreciate it. Many times, that requires thinking outside the box of clubs and dive bars.

TAKING THE FIRST STEP

It's exciting to consider the possibility of making a living off of our music. The goal of supporting ourselves and our passion may be the same from musician to musician, but the way to getting there will be as different as the music we each create. No two songwriters tread the same path towards success, so it can be difficult to understand how to go about reaching our goals without a clear roadmap. The independent songwriter is an entrepreneur, responsible for creating, defining, and marketing our own music. We're not only marketing our music, we're marketing ourself, and it takes time to develop the awareness and business skills we need to carve our way through the jungle of the industry.

When I began my career, my goal was to get paid to write songs. I learned quickly that I couldn't just walk into a record label or music publisher and toss my tape on the desk of an A&R guy and hope to get discovered. I would have to find a way to meet the people who needed the skills I was developing. Funny enough, almost two decades later, that is still how I'd describe my day-to-day job as a writer and artist.

So what are the steps to meeting the people who need your skills? The answer is unique to each writer and artist, but there are some questions you can ask yourself to start whittling down the answers. Let's take a look at how you might define the skills you have and the music you create, and how you might approach connecting that with the world of music around you.

WHO ARE YOU?

The music we create so often reflects qualities of who we are as people. Taking inventory of the emotion our songs convey, and the emotional responses of people who listen to and enjoy our songs, is a great way to understand who we are as artists. I used to think I had to conform my songwriting to what was popular at the moment. The problem with this is that instead of letting what I naturally create point to who will connect with and then benefit from it, I tried to become whatever I thought anyone wanted my songs to be. This affected not only the songs I tried to write, but the gigs I tried to book and the people I tried to network with. I kept coming up against resistance, finally recognizing that I didn't enjoy the music I was creating, or the circles I was hanging out in. It wasn't until I let go of the need for my music to fulfill an expectation that I was able to let it flourish into the best it could be.

Discovering who we are as artists is part of designing our brand. Our brand consists of our sound, image, and what we stand for. Our brand is what people associate with. To begin understanding and developing your brand, you'll need to dare to focus. For your music to be very well liked by some, it will also be very un-liked by others, and for others still, they won't have strong feelings for you at all. To get started defining what your songs and what you as an artist will say, you'll be working within each of these four broad areas below.

1. Write

Continuing to write songs even as you take care of business aspects of your craft is very important to defining who we are, and growing as artists. Every so often in the midst of the writing process, try to choose three of your original songs that you feel strongly about. Listen to them one at a time, and let your mind go back to the place you were when you wrote them. After each song, journal for a few pages on what sparked the song idea, what message you really want the listener to know from the song, and any other feelings and thoughts that come up when you think about the song. Set the journals aside for a few days before bringing them out again. As you read what you wrote, highlight any words, phrases, or sentences that seem to really capture what you were feeling and thinking. Trust your initial instincts, and try not to doubt yourself.

2. Perform

Play live or a recording of three of your original songs for two or three people you trust. These can be family or friends, or even people you just met, but they should be willing and able to reflect back to you what they felt in response to the song. Help them to describe their feelings with adjectives. You might give them a list of adjectives like the one at www.grammar.yourdictionary.com so they can circle the ones that apply. Ask them what they thought was the main message of the song. Ask them what kinds or groups of people they think might really connect with your songs. This information can be helpful in forming a picture of what we're offering to the listener, both with our personality and what we stand for, and professionally with our musical sound. We can use this to develop our image and music further.

3. Work with a Producer

Working with a producer who can visualize your songs in the scope of an arrangement is a great way to help define our music more. The process of recording our songs forces us to commit to musical decisions, and in great songwriter/producer collaborations, it broadens our understanding of how our music can be arranged. For articles and ideas on how to find and work with a producer, please visit my blog at www.songwritingtips.net.

4. Network

Much of our time as writers and artists is spent meeting and forming relationships with fans and people working in the music business. The connections we make early on in our career can be long lasting and foundational to the opportunities that find us and the ones we make later on. We meet people everywhere we go, with every activity we're involved in. When we're more clear on the kind of music we create and who would like to listen to and buy that music, we can become clearer on where to meet those people. One of the first steps of networking is identifying where the music we like to create is played. It may be a venue, such as a club, but it may be a bookstore or an outdoor festival or a fundraising event. It may be an organization online that promotes the same message our music conveys, and forming a relationship with that organization opens the door to promoting our music through that organization's activities. Many times, we don't know how a relationship is going to serve us or the other person in the future. The opportunities that arise from our networking often come very organically. A respectful, positive attitude that shows we're interested in helping others at the same time as helping ourselves opens doors we didn't even know existed.

Enjoy the journey as you express yourself musically. You'll be learning as you go, and each day can bring opportunities to write, record, perform, and connect with others in ways you never planned or expected. The rewards are lifelong, and life changing, if you let them be. Above all, know that each day you do the best you can with what you have. And if you're dedicated to doing your best, what you have is the potential to deeply affect others with the art that is uniquely you.

A. GLOSSARY

arpeggio. Chord tones that are played sequentially rather than simultaneously.

beats per minute (bpm). The measurement of the speed of the song.

borrowed chords. Chords outside the written key.

bridge. The song section that often follows the second chorus. It may be instrumental or lyrical, carry a new or broken-down version of the groove, and functions to provide our ears with a fresh sound before the final chorus.

chord chart. Notation showing harmony and sometimes distinct rhythms that an instrumentalist reads to play the song.

chord progression. A sequence of chords.

chord tone. A note included in a chord.

chord voicing. A specific ordering of chord tones.

chorus. The song section that summarizes the main point and often contains the title of the song.

diatonic. "Of the scale." Notes and chords that are derived from the key signature.

dominant. The name for the fifth tone degree of a scale.

downbeat. The first beat of a measure.

ear training/aural skills. The skill by which musicians identify—solely by hearing—elements of music such as pitches, intervals, melody, chords, and rhythms.

flat (♭). A symbol indicating a half step below the note.

harmonic contrast. Changing the chord or frequency with which we play the chords to give a new section of the song a distinct sound.

harmony. The chords that support the melody.

internal repetition. Repeating a portion of or the whole lyrical phrase.

interval. The distance between two notes.

intro. The song section that introduces the song's groove, and often carries the melodic motif in a lead instrument before the verse begins.

key. Tonic note and chord that is felt as the song's pitch "center."

measure or bar. A segment of time defined by a given number of beats. For example, one measure of 4/4 time is four quarter notes long.

melody. The notes we sing, or hear played in the lead instrument.

metaphor. Seeing one thing as another, such as "crunchy conversation" or "tired words."

motive or motif. A short melodic or lyrical fragment that gives the song its unique sound or identity.

musical phrase. A group of melodic notes or a harmonic progression that has a beginning and end. Phrases, just like sentences, feel closed when they are finished. Longer musical phrases, like verbal sentences, are made up of smaller phrases.

neighbor note. A diatonic note just above or just below a chord tone.

non-diatonic. Chords and notes that are outside the key signature.

odd meter. An unusual time signature, such as 7/8, 9/8, or 11/4.

outro. The song's closing section or ending, often restating the groove and melodic motif that is most prominent in the song.

passing note. A diatonic note in between two chord tones.

phrase. A lyrical or musical unit that is a complete musical thought.

pickup. Melody notes that begin a phrase before the downbeat.

pitch. An individual musical note.

prechorus. The song section just before the chorus section. It's function may be to "ramp up" energy towards the chorus, tell any story that is necessary to know before the chorus, or simply provide contrast by taking our ear somewhere new between the verse and chorus.

rhythm. Note duration.

scale. An ordered sequence of notes within an octave.

score. The musical notation of the melody, harmony, and arrangement on multiple staves.

sensory writing. Descriptive journaling using our senses of taste, touch, sight, sound, smell, and movement.

sharp (♯). A symbol indicating a half step above the note.

song form. The order of the sections that make up the song, including verses, prechoruses, choruses, bridges, etc.

song sections. The distinct formal components of a song including verse, chorus, prechorus, bridge, etc..

song skeleton. The melody, harmony, and lyrics that make up the song. Does not include arrangement or production ideas.

staff. Five lines where we write notes and rhythms.

subdominant. The fourth degree of a scale.

tempo. The speed of the song.

tense. A verb form indicating time, such as present, past, and future. It is helpful to the listener to keep the tense consistent to establish "when" the song is happening.

time signature. A symbol indicating how many beats are in each measure and which note value constitutes one beat.

tonic. The tonal center or final resolution tone.

triad. A chord made up of three notes. Usually the root, 3, and 5.

verse. The song section that develops the story.

verse/refrain. A song form that uses a single refrain line instead of a chorus.

B. SONG LISTENING EXAMPLES

Artist	Title	Songwriter(s)
Sara Bareilles	"Love Song"	Sara Bareilles
	"Basket Case"	Sara Bareilles
Beyoncé	"If I Were a Boy"	BC Jean and Toby Gad
B.o.B.	"Airplanes"	"B.o.B., Kinetics & One Love, Alex da Kid, DJ Frank E, Christine Dominguez
Rascal Flatts	"Life Is a Highway"	Tom Cochrane
The Guess Who	"American Woman"	Randy Bachman, Burton Cummings, Garry Peterson, and Jim Kale
Calvin Harris	"Summer"	Calvin Harris
	"Feel So Close"	Calvin Harris
Michael Jackson	"Bad"	Michael Jackson
Avril Lavigne	"I'm with You"	Avril Lavigne, Lauren Christy, Scott Spock, Graham Edwards
Cyndi Lauper	"Time After Time"	Cyndi Lauper, Rob Hyman
John Legend	"All of Me"	John Legend and Toby Gad
	"Ordinary People"	John Legend and will.i.am

Artist	Title	Songwriter(s)
John Mayer	"Daughters""	John Mayer
	"Gravity"	John Mayer
	"Your Body Is a Wonderland"	John Mayer
	"Say"	John Mayer
Paramore	"Decode"	Hayley Williams, Josh Farro, Taylor York
Katy Perry	"Unconditionally"	Katy Perry, Dr. Luke, Max Martin, Cirkut
	"Firework"	Katy Perry, Mikkel S. Eriksen, Tor Erik Hermansen, Sandy Vee, Ester Dean
	"Dark Horse"	Katy Perry, Juicy J, Max Martin, Cirkut, Dr. Luke, Sarah Hudson
Rihanna	"Unfaithful"	Shaffer "Ne-Yo" Smith, Mikkel S. Eriksen, Tor Erik Hermansen
	"Take a Bow"	Shaffer "Ne-Yo" Smith, Mikkel S. Eriksen, Tor Erik Hermansen
Ed Sheeran	"Sing"	Ed Sheeran, Pharrell Williams
	"Give Me Love"	Ed Sheeran, Jake Gosling, Chris Leonard
Taylor Swift	"Red"	Taylor Swift
	"22"	Taylor Swift, Max Martin, Shellback
Carrie Underwood	"Good Girl"	Carrie Underwood, Ashley Gorley, Chris DeStefano
	"Before He Cheats"	Chris Tompkins, Josh Kear

C. SONGWRITER RESOURCES

Online

Articles and video tutorials on the craft and business of songwriting by Andrea Stolpe. **www. songwritingtips.net**

The American Society of Composers, Authors and Publishers (ASCAP). **www.ascap.com**

Broadcast Music Incorporated (BMI). **www.bmi.com**

Nashville Songwriters Association International (NSAI). **www.nashvillesongwriters.com**

Songwriters Guild of America. **www.songwritersguild.com**

Association of Independent Music Publishers (AIMP). **www.aimp.org**

Pat Pattison. **www.patpattison.com**

Berklee Online. **online.berklee.edu**

Taxi, an independent A&R company. **www.taxi.com**

Object Writing, Prose, and Poetry Forum. **www.objectwriting.com**

Production and Engineering Services. **www.sonicartproductions.com**

SongWork, a songwriting education site featuring unlimited access to video lectures by nationally-acclaimed teachers including Steve Seskin, Pat Pattison, Andrea Stolpe, Steve Leslie, Jimmy Kachulis, and Bonnie Hayes. **www.songwork.com**

Books

Songwriting

Braheny, John. *The Craft and Business of Songwriting.* Writer's Digest Books, 2006.

Pattison, Pat. *Songwriting Without Boundaries: Lyric Writing Exercises for Finding Your Voice.* Writer's Digest Books, 2011.

—*Writing Better Lyrics.* Writer's Digest Books, 2009.

—*Songwriting: Essential Guide to Rhyming 2ⁿᵈ Ed.* Boston: Berklee Press, 2014.

Stolpe, Andrea. *Popular Lyric Writing.* Boston: Berklee Press, 2007.

Voice

Allen, Jeffrey. Various titles.

Gagné, Jeannie. *Your Singing Voice*. Boston: Berklee Press, 2012.

Peckham, Anne. *The Contemporary Singer 2nd Ed.* Boston: Berklee Press, 2010.

Piano/Keyboard

Harrison, Mark. Various titles. **www.harrisonmusic.com**

Schmeling, Paul, and Dave Limina. *Instant Keyboard.* Boston: Berklee Press, 2002.

Schmeling, Paul, and Russell Hoffmann. *The Berklee Practice Method: Keyboard.* Boston: Berklee Press, 2001.

Guitar

Baione, Larry. *The Berklee Practice Method: Guitar.* Boston: Berklee Press, 2001.

Fujita, Tomo. *Instant Guitar.* Boston: Berklee Press, 2002.

Leavitt, William. *Berklee Basic Guitar (series).* Boston: Berklee Press, 1986.

—*A Modern Method for Guitar Vol. 1 with Online Video.* Video lessons with Larry Baione. Boston: Berklee Press, 2014.

Peckham, Rick. *Berklee Rock Guitar Chord Dictionary.* Boston: Berklee Press, 2010.

ABOUT THE AUTHOR

Photo by Jon Hastings

Andrea Stolpe is a songwriter and music educator. For two decades she has worked as a staff writer for music publishing companies such as EMI, Almo-Irving, and Universal. Author of the Berklee Online course *Commercial Songwriting Techniques* and book *Popular Lyric Writing*, Andrea's passion is helping writers at all levels write to their highest potential. She lives in Los Angeles, where she teaches songwriting at Berklee Online and the University of Southern California, and coaches songwriters locally and remotely in conjunction with Sonic Art Productions. www.andreastolpe.com

Jan Stolpe is a recording engineer, writer, producer, and clinician. He is the founder of Sonic Art Productions, a company designed to help writers and recording artists refine their songs, define their sound, and identify their position in the broader music market. Jan's passion also extends to providing musicians with tools for achieving life-balance between touring, writing, and home life. Jan lives in Los Angeles. www.sonicartproductions.com

More Fine Publications
from BERKLEE PRESS

ROOTS MUSIC

BEYOND BLUEGRASS

Beyond Bluegrass Banjo
by Dave Hollander and Matt Glaser
50449610 Book/CD $19.99

Beyond Bluegrass Mandolin
by John McGann and Matt Glaser
50449609 Book/CD $19.99

Bluegrass Fiddle and Beyond
by Matt Glaser
50449602 Book/CD $19.99

THE IRISH CELLO BOOK
by Liz Davis Maxfield
50449652 Book/CD $24.99

BERKLEE PRACTICE METHOD

GET YOUR BAND TOGETHER
With additional volumes for other
instruments, plus a teacher's guide.
Bass
50449427 Book/CD $14.95
Drum Set
50449429 Book/CD $14.95
Guitar
50449426 Book/CD $16.99
Keyboard
50449428 Book/CD $14.95

WELLNESS

MANAGE YOUR STRESS AND PAIN THROUGH MUSIC
by Dr. Suzanne B. Hanser and
Dr. Susan E. Mandel
50449592 Book/CD $29.99

MUSICIAN'S YOGA
by Mia Olson
50449587 Book............................. $14.99

THE NEW MUSIC THERAPIST'S HANDBOOK – 2ND ED.
by Dr. Suzanne B. Hanser
50449424 Book............................ $29.95

EAR TRAINING, MUSIC THEORY, IMPROVISATION

BEGINNING EAR TRAINING
by Gilson Schachnik
50449548 Book/CD $16.99

THE BERKLEE BOOK OF JAZZ HARMONY
by Joe Mulholland & Tom Hojnacki
00113755 Book/CD...................... $24.99

THE BERKLEE DICTIONARY OF CONTEMPORARY MUSIC
by Dr. Kari Juusela
00122072.......................................$24.99

BERKLEE MUSIC THEORY – 2ND ED.
by Paul Schmeling
50449615 Rhythm, Scales Intervals:
          Book/CD $24.99
50449616 Harmony: Book/CD .. $22.99

A GUIDE TO JAZZ IMPROVISATION
by John LaPorta
Book/CD Packs
50449439 C Instruments $19.95

IMPROVISATION FOR CLASSICAL MUSICIANS
by Eugene Friesen with Wendy M.
Friesen
50449637 Book/CD $24.99

REHARMONIZATION TECHNIQUES
by Randy Felts
50449496 Book............................ $29.95

MUSIC BUSINESS

HOW TO GET A JOB IN THE MUSIC INDUSTRY - 3RD ED.
by Keith Hatschek
with Breanne Beseda
00130699 Book............................ $27.99

MAKING MUSIC MAKE MONEY
by Eric Beall
50448009 Book............................ $26.95

MUSIC MARKETING
by Mike King
50449588 Book $24.99

MUSIC INDUSTRY FORMS
by Jonathan Feist
00121814 Book............................ $14.99

PROJECT MANAGEMENT FOR MUSICIANS
by Jonathan Feist
50449659 Book $27.99

THE SELF-PROMOTING MUSICIAN – 3RD EDITION
by Peter Spellman
00119607 Book............................ $24.99

MUSIC PRODUCTION & ENGINEERING

AUDIO MASTERING
by Jonathan Wyner
50449581 Book/CD $29.99

AUDIO POST PRODUCTION
by Mark Cross
50449627 Book............................ $19.99

MIX MASTERS
by Maureen Droney
50448023 Book $24.95

PRODUCING AND MIXING HIP-HOP/R&B
by Mike Hamilton
50449555 Book/DVD-ROM $19.99

PRODUCING DRUM BEATS
by Eric Hawkins
50449598 Book/CD-ROM Pack $22.99

UNDERSTANDING AUDIO
by Daniel M. Thompson
50449456 Book $24.99

Prices subject to change without notice.
Visit your local music dealer or bookstore,
or go to **www.berkleepress.com**

Berklee Press Publications feature material developed at the Berklee College of Music.

SONGWRITING, COMPOSING, ARRANGING

ARRANGING FOR LARGE JAZZ ENSEMBLE
by Dick Lowell and Ken Pullig
50449528 Book/CD $39.95

COMPLETE GUIDE TO FILM SCORING – 2ND ED.
by Richard Davis
50449607 .... $27.99

MELODY IN SONGWRITING
by Jack Perricone
50449419 Book/CD...................... $24.95

MODERN JAZZ VOICINGS
by Ted Pease and Ken Pullig
50449485 Book/CD...................... $24.95

MUSIC COMPOSITION FOR FILM AND TELEVISION
by Lalo Schifrin
50449604 Book............................ $34.99

MUSIC NOTATION
PREPARING SCORES AND PARTS
by Matthew Nicholl and
Richard Grudzinski
50449540 Book............................ $16.99

MUSIC NOTATION
THEORY AND TECHNIQUE FOR MUSIC NOTATION
by Mark McGrain
50449399 Book $24.95

POPULAR LYRIC WRITING
by Andrea Stolpe
50449553 Book............................ $14.95

SONGWRITING: ESSENTIAL GUIDE
by Pat Pattison
50481582 Lyric and Form Structure:
          Book.......................... $16.99
00124366 Rhyming: Book –
          2nd Ed. $16.99

SONGWRITING STRATEGIES
by Mark Simos
50449621 Book/Online Audio... $22.99

THE SONGWRITER'S WORKSHOP
by Jimmy Kachulis
50449519 Harmony: Book/CD . $29.95

AUTOBIOGRAPHY

LEARNING TO LISTEN: THE JAZZ JOURNEY OF GARY BURTON
by Gary Burton
00117798 Book............................ $27.99

HAL•LEONARD®
CORPORATION
7777 W. BLUEMOUND RD. P.O. BOX 13819
MILWAUKEE, WISCONSIN 53213

0415

 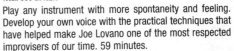

Guitar Books and DVDs
from Berklee Press

BEBOP GUITAR SOLOS
- by Michael Kaplan
00121703 Book $14.99

BERKLEE BLUES GUITAR SONGBOOK
- by Michael Williams
50449593 Book/CD $24.99

BLUES GUITAR TECHNIQUE
- by Michael Williams
50449623 Book/CD $24.99

BERKLEE GUITAR CHORD DICTIONARY
- by Rick Peckham
50449546 Book – Jazz $10.99
50449596 Book – Rock $12.99

BERKLEE JAZZ STANDARDS FOR SOLO GUITAR
- by John Stein
50449653 Book/CD $19.99

THE CHORD FACTORY
Build Your Own Guitar Chord Dictionary
- by Jon Damian
50449541 Book $24.95

THE GUITARIST'S GUIDE TO COMPOSING AND IMPROVISING
- by Jon Damian
50449497 Book/CD $24.95

CREATIVE CHORDAL HARMONY FOR GUITAR
Using Generic Modality Compression
- by Mick Goodrick and Tim Miller
50449613 Book/CD $19.99

FUNK/R&B GUITAR
Creative Solos, Grooves & Sounds
- by Thaddeus Hogarth
50449569 Book/CD $19.95

JOE STUMP'S GUITAR CHOP SHOP
Building Rock/Metal Technique
- by Joe Stump
50449601 Book/CD $19.99

CHOP BUILDER FOR ROCK GUITAR
featuring Shred Lord Joe Stump
50448015 DVD $19.95

JAZZ IMPROVISATION FOR GUITAR
- by Garrison Fewell
50449503 Book/CD – A Melodic Approach $24.99
50449594 Book/CD – A Harmonic Approach $24.99

A MODERN METHOD FOR GUITAR
- by William Leavitt

VOLUME 1: BEGINNER
50449400 Book $14.95
50449404 Book/CD $22.95
50448065 Book/DVD-ROM $34.99

VOLUME 2: INTERMEDIATE
50449410 Book $14.95

VOLUME 3
50449420 Book $16.95

1, 2, 3 COMPLETE
50449468 Book $34.95

JAZZ SONGBOOK
50449539 Book/CD $14.99

ROCK SONGBOOK
50449624 Book/CD $17.99

PLAYING THE CHANGES: GUITAR
A Linear Approach to Improvising
- by Mitch Seidman and Paul Del Nero
50449509 Book/CD $19.95

THE PRACTICAL JAZZ GUITARIST
Essential Tools for Soloing, Comping and Performing
- by Mark White
50449618 Book/CD $19.99

THE PRIVATE GUITAR STUDIO HANDBOOK
Strategies and Policies for a Profitable Music Business
- by Mike McAdam
00121641 Book $14.99

Visit your local music dealer or bookstore,
or go to **www.berkleepress.com**

Prices and availability subject to change without notice

For more information about Berklee Press
or Berklee College of Music, contact us:

1140 Boylston Street
Boston, MA 02215-3693
www.berkleepress.com

7777 W. BLUEMOUND RD. P.O. BOX 13819 MILWAUKEE, WI 53213

0314